THE SANDLAPPER STORE, INC.

D1558095

SOUTHERN FISH AND SEAFOOD COOKBOOK

BY - JAN WONGREY

ILLUSTRATED BY LAURA PECK

Dedication

The spoon I was born with was certainly not of silver, but it was a spoon—a cooking spoon.

I was born the son of a European who became a restaurateur and who introduced me to the noble art of cooking. I was also very close to an uncle whose passion for fishing outweighed all reasoning; he instructed me in the gentle and contemplative art of fishing.

To them both—Matthew Wongrey and Rowland "Pappy" Newman—I dedicate this book.

FIRST EDITION, 1975
SECOND EDITION, 1980

Copyright © 1975 by THE SANDLAPPER STORE, INC.

INTERNATIONAL STANDARD BOOK NUMBER: 0-87844-026-7

Published by
THE SANDLAPPER STORE, INC.
P.O. Box 841 • Lexington, S.C. 29072

Manufactured in the United States of America

Contents

The Author

Now a free lance writer, Jan Wongrey was Outdoors Editor for
The State newspaper for 5½ years, was awarded the 1970 Conserva-
tion Communications Award and in September of 1974 was awarded
Best Newspaper Column Award for the Southeast by the South-
eastern Outdoor Press Association. He is also a past director of the
Southeastern Outdoor Press Association.

Wongrey has been published in **Field & Stream, Southern Out-
doors, Sport Fishing, Wheels Afield, Camping Guide, South
Carolina Wildlife, Rotarian, Islander, Lowcountry Sportsman, North
Carolina Wildlife, Bassmaster** and **Sandlapper.**

Reared in a restaurant family, Wongrey had six years cooking experience before embarking on a writing career. Many of his published stories have dealt with fish and game recipes.

Wongrey presently writes a weekly outdoor column for the Southeast Farm Press which is distributed throughout the southeastern
states.

Introduction

To spend a morning or afternoon catching fish, then return home physically drained but mentally refreshed and take what I have caught and enjoy it in its simplest form (or create a culinary spectacular from it) is, to me, the ultimate in enjoyment. If I can instill in others my delight in catching and cooking fish, this book will have served its purpose.

In the pages to follow, I discuss the basic methods of fish cookery. The following descriptions will aid in understanding the techniques discussed.

BROILING

I broil fillets, whole dressed fish and steaks four inches from the coils. The rule of thumb is to broil fillets five to eight minutes per side; whole dressed fish five minutes per pound; and steaks five to eight minutes per side. But rule of thumb is not always adequate, so, as you read, you will find that I have noted to cook until the flesh of the fish begins to flake. A broiled fish should be brought to the table golden and juicy.

BAKING

You will find that the temperature specified for most of the seafood recipes is 350 degrees, and you will find instructions to cook fish until the flesh flakes. Again, your goal should be to have the fish come from the oven lightly browned and succulent.

FRYING

The first-time fish fryer often finds that the fish has not cooked through. This is the result of improper preparation and it is simple to correct. Before frying a fish, score it. This is done by drawing a knife diagonally across the fish two or three times on each side. Each slice should be no more than an eighth of an inch deep. This allows cooking oil to penetrate the meat and also hastens frying time. Too often fried fish needlessly come from the pan dry and tasteless.

You should also let excess oil drain from fish before serving. The most popular method for draining fried fish—in fact, all fried foods— is to place them on paper towels. This, of course, will help but you are allowing the bottom fish to soak up oil. This can be alleviated by placing fish on a wire rack. A pie pan or several paper towels placed under the rack will catch the oil. A minor but important task when seeking the ultimate in fried fish.

If frying fish in an electric fry pan, cooking oil should be heated on low heat and gradually increased to 375 or 380 degrees before fish are entered. Fry fish three to five minutes per side.

I, personally, am somewhat of a traditionalist when it comes to frying fish. I favor the cast-iron skillet.

Shortening

  (1) Heat shortening on low heat until melted.
  (2) Place on high heat until shortening begins to bubble.
  (3) Enter Fish.
  (4) Reduce to medium heat and cook 3 to 5 minutes per side.

Cooking Oil

  (1) On high heat, heat cooking oil until it begins to bubble.
  (2) Enter fish.
  (3) Reduce to medium heat and cook 3 to 5 minutes per side.

POACHING

Poaching is simple and retains the natural fish flavor and protein. A commercial poacher is available for those who prepare seafood, but we can improvise if we must.

In a deep pan, season water with a condiment such as salt, pepper, lemon juice, lime juice, parsley, bay leaves, celery leaves, etc., bring water to boil for two or three minutes and reduce to simmer. Add fish, cover, and cook until flesh flakes when tested with fork.

Another method is as follows: Season water as before, put fish in a cheesecloth and enter into deep pan. Cook until fish flakes when tested with a fork, remove, place fish on serving platter and remove wrapping.

STEAMING

Juices and taste remain at their peak when seafood is cooked in this manner.

(1) If a commercial steaming rack is not available, a deep pan or pot fitted with a colander will suffice.

(2) No more than two inches of water should be placed in pan or pot. Season water (see Poaching) and bring to boil for two or three minutes to activate seasonings. Do not reduce temperature.

(3) Place fish in colander and cover with lid.

(4) Cook until flesh flakes easily with fork.

STEWING

The catfish is the true stewing fish. On the other hand, I do not hesitate to make a stew of bream or redbreasts, largemouth bass and the like. Yet, the catfish has that indefinable something that renders zest to a fish stew.

There is nothing complicated to whipping up a stew. A few grains of this, a few flakes of that, an extra touch of something else will produce a palatable stew. Since stews are most often concocted on riverbanks, in river swamp club houses, at campsites and the like, there is no need to emphasize anything other than that fish stew is one of those outdoorsy dishes that is at its best when you apply the gentle art of southern fish cookery.

Part I

Freshwater Fish

LARGEMOUTH BASS

Gill-flared bass shimmy against a backdrop of moss-clothed cypress tress, vast shallow-water grassbeds and beturtled oxbow lakes. The silence is interrupted only by the sing of mosquitoes, the drone of dragonflies, the wet line leaving the spool and the plug plunking into the water. This is the contemplative order of bass fishing below the Mason-Dixon Line.

Psychological? Maybe. But bass fishing is psychological to an extent and the mystique southern lakes offer is sufficient itself to attract most bass anglers.

Why the South when these fish are prolific in other waters? There is but one answer: size. And size is attributed to the availability of year-round food for these fish. Extreme winter weather is the exception rather than the rule in this semitropic land of palmettos and mimosas. Bass suffer little for food even on the coldest winter days.

Spring comes early and winter, when and if it arrives, is short lived. Summer continues far beyond the calendar limitations. A utopia, no, but the climate is more than harmonious with the habits of the fisherman.

1

The southern largemouth is unquestionably truculent. Not as atrocious as the bluefish with its slashing teeth, but savage in the respect that he is the ruler in what, to the eye, seems an endless realm of tranquility. Yet, beneath this serene exterior of waxen water lilies, clusters of fragrant wild azaleas and turtles sunning on crumbling logs lives the rampaging largemouth. After reaching two pounds, maybe less, he becomes lord of his domain, an absolute monarch.

The largemouth develops an insatiable appetite for insects, baitfish, game fish, frogs and snakes — even ducklings, and flightless young birds beat from their nests by heavy spring rains or gale force winds. He is as diurnal as he is nocturnal, feeding when he wants and eating as much as required to fill his sagging paunch. He, in short, is a glutton and his nickname of "hawg" is deserving.

The southern largemouth is a product of his environment — big, temperamental, aggressive and vehement as he prowls the shallows, haunts deeps pools and lies in wait beneath the overhang of shoreline growth. The unrestrained spirit with which this fish feeds is not rumor but fact, and such habits offer the bass angler unlimited versatility. The options of how one chooses to catch it are endless and the pleasures many.

Of all freshwater fish in the country, the largemouth is the most sought after, for its value as a food fish equals its merits as a sport fish. It offers the cook as much versatility as it offers the fisherman: It can be fried, broiled, boiled, baked and stewed, as the following recipes will indicate.

BAKED BASS WITH TOMATOES

1 3- to 4-lb bass ready to cook
1 No. 303 can tomatoes
2 slices uncooked breakfast bacon
1 small onion, chopped
2 cups water
1 rib celery, chopped
2 T. concentrated lemon juice
Salt and pepper to taste

Rub fish with lemon juice. Sprinkle with salt and pepper. Arrange bacon across fish and place in baking pan. Add remaining ingredients. Place in oven preheated to 350 degrees. Cook fish 5 minutes per pound each side or until fish flakes when tested with fork. When done, place fish on a large platter and pour pan juices over it. Serves 4.

BROILED BASS IN ITALIAN DRESSING

This recipe is especially good with bass fillets or whole cleaned fish weighing 1½ to 2½ pounds.

4 fillets
½ cup bottled Italian dressing

Marinate fillets for 30 minutes in Italian dressing. Remove, place on cookie sheet or in broiler pan and broil 4 inches from coils, 5 to 8 minutes per side. (All fish should be broiled 4 inches from coils.) Serves 4.

BUTTERMILK BASS FILLETS

See Introduction concerning frying fish:

6 fillets
1 cup buttermilk
1 cup cracker or corn meal

Salt and pepper fillets to taste, dip in buttermilk and dust with meal. Fry 3 to 5 minutes per side.

BASS-CHEESE CASSEROLE

6 fillets
1 egg
½ cup sweet milk
1 cup cheddar cheese, grated
Cracker or corn meal

Salt and pepper fillets. Dip in egg beaten with milk and dust with meal. Place fillet in casserole dish and bake in preheated 400 degree oven 10 to 12 minutes. Turn fillets, top with cheese and bake 10 to 12 minutes more. Serves 6.

FOIL-BAKED FILLETS

4 fillets
½ stick of margarine or butter
Juice from 2 fresh lemons or 2 T. lemon concentrate
1 t. cooking sherry

Melt margarine in saucepan. Add lemon juice, sherry. Stir. Remove from heat and let cool. Marinate fish in this sauce for 20 to 30 minutes. Salt and pepper and wrap individual fillets in aluminum foil. Place on oven rack and bake at 400 degrees, 5 to 8 minutes per side, or until meat flakes when tested with fork. Serves 4. (This recipe can also be used for charcoal grill cookery.)

SKILLET-FRIED BASS

Select fillets or whole cleaned bass weighing ½ pound to 1½ pounds. Preheat skillet (see Introduction for frying) or electric fry pan until vegetable oil or shortening begins to bubble. Salt and pepper fish to taste, dust lightly with cracker or corn meal or flour and fry 3 to 5 minutes per side. Meat should be moist, not dry.

Remember, when frying fish, after oil has cooled, pour into a glass or metal container for further usage. Cooking oil tends to fry better when used a second or third time.

CATFISH

As a youngster, we trapped them for spending money and did quite well. Later, we found them to be one of the most sporting fish ever to rip line from a spool. We know of few fishermen who cannot attest to their strength; even the small ones, half-pounders, possess remarkable hitting, running and staying power when a fisherman's honed hook slips through the bait and becomes embedded in them.

We are speaking of the catfish and there are many varieties to choose from: channel cat, blue cat, flathead, white, brown bullhead, yellow bullhead and black bullhead.

Catfishing has evolved from the calendar scene of a boy sitting by an idle stream with canepole to that of the adult fisherman using sophisticated fishing gear and techniques. However, we are still quite fond of the contemplative creek scene of old and continue to fish with canepole when time allows.

There are many reasons why the catfish has gained popularity: The continuing growth of fishing and the construction of new fishing reservoirs, plus the transplanting of various species from one state to another, have increased their numbers and, correspondingly, their popularity.

We know of no other fish that will hit a wider assortment of baits and plugs than the catfish. We have caught them with worms, crickets, live minnows, dead minnows, crawfish, small frogs, bass bugs, bream bugs, topwater plugs, underwater plugs and spoons.

Catfish have long been sold commercially but their distribution has been limited. While they have been widely favored for years in the deep southern states, elsewhere, until recently, marketing attempts have been meager. But now an almost nationwide catfish farming program has established a market and matching appetite. Like country music, the fish has now been accepted and it has become chic to ask for catfish when dining out.

(A thought: we have often wondered had the catfish been given another name would its fighting and eating merits have been more rapidly acclaimed?)

As this is being written, we can smell the spicy aroma of a catfish stew simmering. We know of few smells as inviting. While the catfish can be fried, baked and broiled, it is the stewed catfish which provides the ultimate treat. Some diners prefer the white stew, others the red. Some insist on having the meat removed from the bones and concocted into a chowder. Some like the stew served on rice; others like it ladled across grits. Still others prefer it with neither rice nor grits. We have tried it various ways and have never been able to pick a favorite.

(Refer to Cleaning and Freezing Fish for information on preparing catfish for cooking.)

RED CATFISH STEW

- 3 lbs. skinned catfish
- 1 cup onion, chopped
- 2 T. bacon fat
- 2 cups ketchup or 1 can of tomato soup or 1 No. 303 can tomatoes
- 2 cups diced uncooked potatoes
- 1 T. Worcestershire sauce

Cook onion in bacon fat. Remove and empty cooked onions into a colander to strain unwanted fat. In pot, layer salt-and-peppered catfish with onions, potatoes, ketchup and Worcestershire sauce. Repeat layers. Add water until it covers top layer. Cover pot, bring to a boil, then reduce heat to simmer and cook until potatoes are done. (Tabasco sauce may be added if you prefer a hot stew.) Fish stews are quick cooking. Remove from heat and allow to cool for at least an hour. This gives the stew's seasonings time to blossom. Reheat slowly before serving. Serves 4 to 6.

WHITE CATFISH STEW

Prepare as above, replacing the tomato base and water with a quart of sweet milk.

BROTH OR CLEAR CATFISH STEW

3 lbs. skinned catfish
1 cup onion, chopped
2 t. salt
1 t. black pepper

Place ingredients in pot, cover with water, bring to boil. Reduce to simmer and cook 20 to 30 minutes. Serves 4 to 6.

CATFISH-MUSHROOM STEW

Prepare as for Red Stew, using 2 cans condensed mushroom soup and 2 cans water instead of ketchup or tomato soup or canned tomatoes.

CATFISH CHOWDER

Sometimes served as a stew, sometimes as a chowder, it can either be red, white, clear or flavored with mushrooms, depending upon preference. However, a chowder, unlike a stew, is cooked with flaked meat rather than whole or chunked meat. The following recipe is for red chowder using ketchup.

2 lbs. ready-to-cook catfish
1 cup onion, chopped
2 t. salt
1 t. pepper

Place ingredients into pot, cover with water and bring to a boil. Cover with lid, place on simmer and cook until meat begins to flake. Remove fish, let cool and strip meat from bones. Flake meat with fingers and place back into pot.

Add:

2 cups diced uncooked potatoes
2 cups ketchup

Bring to boil, cover, reduce to simmer and cook until fork can easily be inserted into potatoes. You may want to add 1 tablespoon Worcestershire sauce or 1 teaspoon Tabasco sauce. Or both. Serves 6 to 8.

Sometimes a stew cooked with ketchup tastes too strongly of ketchup. This can be dealt with by adding 1 tablespoon of white vinegar to help neutralize the strong ketchup taste.

FRIED BREADED CATFISH

Season whole cleaned catfish or fish steaks with salt and pepper. For variation and an unusual-but-zesty flavor, rub fish before seasoning with a clove of garlic. Dust fish with either cracker or corn meal or flour and fry in preheated pan, 3 to 5 minutes per side. Vegetable oil or shortening should be at least ½ to 1 inch deep in pan. Packaged cornbread mix is also an excellent breading ingredient.

If you have a deep-fat fryer, try this method. Beat 2 eggs with 1 pint sweet milk. Place cracker meal in one bowl and flour in another. Salt and pepper fish, dust lightly with cracker meal. Then dip in egg mixture and dust with flour. This coating is very palatable.

This catfish could be cooked in your kitchen skillet or electric fry pan if the fish are small or filleted, but we prefer a deep-fat fryer for cooking breaded fish.

BAKED CATFISH

1 3- to 4-lb. whole cleaned catfish
4 strips breakfast bacon
1 onion, chopped
1 cup water

Salt and pepper fish to taste. Wrap with bacon; place in baking pan with onion and water. Bake 5 minutes per pound each side in 350 degree oven or until meat flakes when tested with fork. Serves 4. (For stuffed catfish, see Breads and Stuffings.)

REDBREAST

In our home state of South Carolina the Black, Little Pee Dee, Combahee and Edisto rivers flow deep in the Low Country. In this contagious land the rivers are black and cypress trees wear long, white moss beards. Squirrels frolic in the tall trees and fidgety wood ducks spring from quiet eddies. There is usually a breeze to bring the woody river scent to your nostrils.

There is a sought after fish within these rivers — not a big fish, but one endowed with the fighter's spirit: the redbreast. If you demand success, it's essential that you know something of this fish before you challenge.

Redbreasts inhabit the entire east coast and westward into Alabama, Mississippi and Texas. But more than likely you bypass them in favor of larger reservoir fish.

Maybe you know them as yellowbreasts, creek robins or yellow-bellies, but their true name is redbreasts. They are a member of the sunfish family and closely resemble one of their cousins, the bream.

The redbreast's most distinguishing characteristic is its long, narrow, black ear flap. The fish is also brilliantly colored, particularly during the spawning season, and the breast of the rooster (male) is orange-red.

Redbreasts reach a maximum length of eight to ten inches. A one-pounder is considered big and only rarely do these fish grow to two pounds. But what they lack in size, they compensate for in fighting ability.

These fish do not particularly thrive in ponds or lakes but prefer fast-running water. Spawning occurs in April and early May. Nests are usually located near the banks in one to three feet of water. Unlike other members of the sunfish family, they do not spawn in great numbers but are rather solitary. Redbreasts feed upon insects, minnows and crawfish. Anglers fish for them with an assortment of baits such as crickets, earthworms, grubworms, catalpa worms, small spinners, small topwater popping bugs and some dry and wet flies.

Favorite haunts are areas where a river eddies to the bank to form small pools. Here also you will find overhangs, spider-webbed cypress roots, stumps, bushes, logs and whatever else there is to tangle your line and sever your patience.

Except when bedding, they are loners and seem to enjoy this solitude: To catch three from a single hole is to be blessed. Although we have heard stories of fishermen pulling ten or fifteen from a given spot, this has not yet been our pleasure.

However finicky and secretive they sometimes appear to the hopeful angler, there is nothing finicky about the fisherman's own appetite when this fish is served. The meat, sometimes as thick as an inch or an inch-and-a-half, is sweet.

PAN-FRIED REDBREAST

See Pan-Fried Bream.

POACHED REDBREASTS WITH LEMON

If you have never before eaten a fish prepared in this manner, you are in for a treat. This method retains both flavor and protein. It is also recommended for those who must refrain from fried foods.

4 whole cleaned redbreasts
2 cups water
1 t. salt
1 bayleaf
1 freshly squeezed lemon or 1 T. lemon concentrate

Place water, salt, bayleaf and lemon juice in pot large enough to hold 4 redbreasts. Cover, bring to boil for 3 minutes. Reduce heat to simmer. Add fish and cook 6 to 10 minutes or until fish flakes when tested with fork. Garnish with fresh parsley and lemon wedges. Serves 4. (For Lemon Sauce, see Sauces to Accompany Fish.)

REDBREASTS WITH MUSTARD

6 fresh river-caught redbreasts
2 T. prepared mustard
1 T. margarine or butter
1 T. lemon juice

Combine all ingredients except fish and heat slowly in saucepan.
Salt and pepper fish to taste. Brush sauce over fish and boil in preheated broiler 4 inches from coils, 5 minutes per side, or until fish
flakes easily when tested with fork. Serves 4 to 6.

REDBREASTS WITH HERB SEASONING

4 whole cleaned redbreasts
8 slices breakfast bacon
Prepared herb seasoning

Salt and pepper to taste. Dust stomach cavity of redbreasts with
herb seasoning. Wrap each fish with two slices bacon. Place on
broiler pan 4 inches from coils. Broil 5 minutes per side or until flesh
flakes when tested with fork. Serves 4.

REDBREAST PATTIES

3 to 4 whole cleaned redbreasts
2 cups water
1 t. salt
½ t. pepper
¼ cup onion, finely chopped

Place fish and remaining ingredients into pot; cover, bring to boil.
Reduce heat to simmer and cook until meat flakes when tested with
fork. Remove fish to platter to cool, then flake meat from bones.
While fish is cooling, prepare the other ingredients as follows:

1 small onion, chopped
2 T. bell pepper, chopped
¼ cup celery, chopped
2 T. vegetable oil
1 fresh lemon or 1 T. concentrated lemon juice
Dash of Tabasco sauce
Dash of Worcestershire sauce
1 unbeaten egg
1 t. prepared mustard
20 saltine crackers, crushed fine
Cracker meal [as required to dust.]

Cook onion, celery and bell pepper in vegetable oil until tender. Do not brown. After this has cooked, empty into mixing bowl; add lemon, Worcestershire and Tabasco sauces, flaked meat, egg, mustard. Combine. Add cracker crumbs, a spoonful at a time, until well mixed. Shape into individual patties, dust with cracker meal and fry in vegetable oil 3 to 5 minutes per side. Serves 4. (Two patties per person.)

BREAM

If there is one fish that can be called the family fish it is the bream. Small boys idle away their summertime hours fishing along blackwater creeks with their fathers. Mothers and daughters try their luck on the banks of quiet, springtime ponds.

Generally referred to as bream (more apt to be pronounced "brim" the farther south one travels), the fish is known by over a dozen names across the country—bluegill, bald bream, blue sunfish, copperhead bream, black bream, etc.

The full moon in May traditionally signals the first spawning of bream, although this ritual can be delayed a week or a month, depending on whether or not the last winter winds have ceased to blow. But by the full moon in May the fisherman has certainly begun thinking of bream.

Crickets, earthworms and catalpa worms are deadly baits for the scrappy fighters, and limits are easily met when the angler locates a bed of those oversized, bluish-black bream that even the most ardent-and-dedicated bass fishermen find hard to resist.

There is no doubt that those first spring weeks provide the greatest catches as the winter-hungry bream eagerly pounce upon the tasty tidbits offered. But as the spring days give way to the hot, muggy summer months, bream retreat to cooler, deep-water hideouts and restrict most of their feeding to early morning and late afternoon hours, continuing on into the night.

It is on such summer nights that the bream enthusiast can take advantage of the feeding bream and make catches that parallel those of springtime fishing. Under a moon of yellow, all the equipment needed is a canepole (with the line about a foot-and-a-half longer than the pole) and a handful of small topwater bugs.

This type of angling also lends itself to great flyrod opportunities, but unless you are fishing in a rather open area, the flyrod can be a bit of a hindrance as nighttime visibility, even with a full moon, is limited.

The belly of the male bream is coppery red in a mature fish and during spawning, while the female has yellowish belly. The bream can be distinguished from its many cousins by the wide and long ear flap, which is entirely black.

The bream is perhaps one of the most tasty of all panfish in the South and is traditionally fried and served with grits. However, the bream can be prepared in many ways. The following recipes are interchangeable for bream, redbreasts, crappies, warmouths and white bass.

FRIED BREAM FILLETS

Yes, bream can be filleted; and yes, even the largest bream will yield a strip of meat only about as long and wide as your first three fingers. Salt and pepper fillets, dust with cracker meal and fry in vegetable oil 2 or 3 minutes per side. When done, fillets should curl in potato chip fashion.

PAN-FRIED BREAM

8 whole ready-to-cook bream
1 cup vegetable oil or shortening
1 cup cracker or corn meal or all-purpose flour
Salt and pepper to taste

In skillet, heat oil on high heat until it bubbles. Salt and pepper fish, dust with corn meal and place in hot oil. Reduce to medium heat and cook 3 to 5 minutes per side. Serves 4.

BROILED BREAM

8 whole ready-to-cook bream
¼ cup melted margarine or butter

Salt and pepper bream and baste with margarine. Place on broiler pan 4 inches from coils and broil 3 to 5 minutes per side. Serves 4.

BREAM WITH PEPPERS, ONIONS, MUSHROOMS

6 ready-to-cook bream
1 small onion, chopped
1 small bell pepper, chopped
1 2-oz. can mushroom stems and pieces [reserve mushroom liquid]
Salt and pepper to taste

Bring cooking oil level to ¼ inch in skillet. Heat on high heat to bubbling; add fish, onions, pepper and mushrooms. Reduce to medium heat and cook 3 to 5 minutes per side, keeping ingredients moving over and around fish while cooking. When done, remove to platter. Heat mushroom liquid in small saucepan and ladle over fish. Serves 6.

PANFISH CHOWDER

4 whole cleaned fish—bream, redbreasts, small crappies, warmouths or small white bass
1 rib celery, chopped
1 small onion, chopped
1 bayleaf
2 t. salt
2 cracked peppercorns
1 large potato, diced
2 slices fat bacon, diced
1 cup sweet milk
1 cup evaporated milk or heavy cream

Place fish, celery, onion, bay leaf, salt and peppercorns in pot and cover ingredients with water. Cover with lid, bring to boil; reduce to simmer and cook 10 minutes or until fish flakes easily with fork. When fish are done, remove, place on platter and strain stock into another pot. Add potatoes to stock, cover, bring to boil. Reduce to medium heat and cook until fork easily pierces potatoes.

While potatoes are cooking, fry fat bacon in skillet until crisp. Remove from pan to drain excess grease. When potatoes are done, add bacon, milk, cream and flaked fish meat to pot. Cover, keep on medium heat for 5 minutes. Spoon chowder into heated bowls for 4 to 6 persons. Serve with crackers.

STRIPED BASS [ROCKFISH]

The Santee River in South Carolina empties into two massive reservoirs, lakes Marion and Moultrie. These two lakes cover 171,400 acres and together have a shoreline of 450 miles.

Although the Santee-Cooper lakes are noted for their variety of gamefish, the fish that has stimulated the most interest is the striped bass (rockfish.) This saltwater fish became landlocked here and made history when it thrived in the freshwater which it normally visited only during spawning.

Basically, the rockfish season is divided into two parts: the schooling months and the annual spring spawning; both are equally as exciting.

Rockfish, as they are called by South Carolina anglers, begin schooling about the middle of November and continue into January if the weather remains mild. There is nothing technical about this phase of rockfishing. The fish are sighted and you go fishing.

The give-away sign is gulls which gather and dip to the surface, picking up stunned baitfish as the stripers feed. Spoons, feathered jigs, shallow-running lures and some topwater plugs are among the baits anglers offer to the feeding fish.

Though South Carolina claims all rights to its landlocked rockfish, it by no means can lay total claim to rockfishing. A true ocean fish, rockfish — known as striped bass once you cross the South Carolina North Carolina Line—range on up into Maine. Though it spawns and is sought in many inland coastal tributaries, this is a fish of the surf, and from North Carolina northward it is hunted as once was the Holy Grail.

Standard surf tackle, and oftentimes freshwater casting gear, is considered fair play for these surf bruisers. Bait? Anything goes, from cut mullet, to shrimp, bloodworms, plugs, jigs and spoons.

Whether or not you choose to call them rockfish or striped bass and search for them in the Santee-Cooper or travel northward to the surf, they are noble fighters and most appetizing cooked in numerous ways.

BAKED ROCKFISH IN WINE

1 4-5 lb. whole cleaned rockfish
2 cups dry sauterne

Salt and pepper fish. Place in baking pan and pour wine over fish. Place into 350 degree oven and cook 5 minutes per pound each side. Baste frequently. When done, place on serving platter and spoon juice over fish. Serves 4 to 6.

ROCKFISH STEAKS

We prefer to steak those rockfish over 6 pounds. Steaks should be at least 1 inch thick. Such cuts present an almost endless selection of cookery.

BROILED ROCKFISH WITH BACON

4 rockfish steaks
4 strips of breakfast bacon

Salt and pepper steaks; wrap with bacon, fasten with toothpicks and place on broiler pan. Broil 5 to 8 minutes per side. Serves 4.

Variation:

4 steaks
¼ cup melted margarine or butter
2 T. lemon or lime juice

Salt and pepper steaks. Combine melted margarine and lemon juice; baste fish and place 4 inches from coils. Broil 5 to 8 minutes per side. Serves 4.

BROILED ROCKFISH FILLETS

2 lbs. fillets, cut in serving-size portions
½ cup vegetable oil
2 T. lemon juice
1 t. salt
Dash black pepper
Paprika

Combine oil, lemon juice, salt and pepper. Baste fish. Sprinkle each portion with paprika. Place on lightly greased broiler pan and broil 4 inches from coils, 5 to 8 minutes per side. Serves 6.

OVEN-FRIED ROCKFISH FILLETS

1 lb. fillets, cut in 4 serving portions
¼ cup sweet milk
½ t. salt
¾ cup toasted bread crumbs
2 T. vegetable oil or melted shortening

Combine milk, salt. Dip fish in mixture and roll in crumbs. Place fish on lightly greased baking pan. Pour oil over each portion. Bake at 450 degrees, 5 to 8 minutes per side, or until fish are brown and flake when tested with fork. Serves 4.

WARMOUTH [MOLLY]

A warmouth (better known as a molly) is not known for his fighting ability. While it is a feat to catch a blue marlin that has been hooked near the back of the throat and is trying to get into the boat and stab you with his raspy sword, a molly surrenders once he is near the surface. About the only harm that can come to you from a molly is to get stabbed by a dorsal fin while freeing the hook.

Home is those places where cypress trees form cathedrals and where the water is inky and the air seeps with a hint of mystery. A molly is quite slow and if he did not select his habitat with care he would surely starve. He does not care for swift water, but lives within reach of a current where food is served without much effort. Submerged brush, log jams, decayed stumps and cypress roots are haunts of a molly. There, near the bottom, he lies and gets fat from too much food and too little exercise.

Although a molly is lazy and not a great fighter, he is not dumb. In fact, he is quite bright when he feels the pinch of the hook. Instead of fleeing with fright, a molly will swim to the bottom and wedge his thick body tightly into the hump of an arched root. He will stay in this position until jerked free by force.

Molly fishing is simple, quiet and there is little worry about having one jump in the boat and stab you. But though you forego the fight inherent in hooking other freshwater fish, you can look forward to dining on the sweet, succulent flesh of the molly.

TANGY BROILED MOLLIES

4 whole cleaned mollies
2 T. lemon juice
¼ cup bottled French dressing
Salt and pepper

In bowl, combine lemon juice and French dressing. Place fish in marinade 1 hour. Remove, salt and pepper and broil 4 inches from coils, 5 to 8 minutes per side, or until fish flakes when tested with fork. Serves 4.

PAN-FRIED MOLLIES WITH LIME AND ONIONS

4 whole cleaned mollies, salt and peppered to taste
2 large onions, thin sliced
3 T. lime juice

For frying directions, see Pan-Fried Bream.

While fish are frying, place onions and lime juice in another skillet and cook on medium heat until onions are tender. Remove and spoon onions across fried fish on serving platter. Serves 4.

MOLLIES WITH SOUR CREAM

4 whole cleaned mollies
¼ cup melted margarine or butter
1 cup sour cream
½ T. pimiento, chopped
1 t. prepared mustard

Salt and pepper mollies; brush with melted margarine and place 4 inches from coils. Broil 5 to 8 minutes per side. Combine sour cream, pimiento and mustard in small bowl. When fish are turned, and just before browning, spoon sour cream mixture over fish and let brown lightly. Remove and serve to 4.

FISH SANDWICH

The fish sandwich has become one of the most popular fast foods of today and is both nutritious and tasty. To prepare, pan fry mollie fillets (2 per sandwich) or other panfish. Drain excess oil. Place on warmed buns or sliced bread. Serve with tartar sauce or relish, pickles, tomatoes and any of your favorite sandwich spreads.

CRAPPIE

Two of the most important freshwater fish in the Southeast are the white and black crappie, also known as white perch, goggle-eyes and sand bass. Generally, the white crappie is classified as a southern fish while the black seems to favor a more northern climate. Yet both fish overlap each other's territory. Spawning and food preferences are the same for both fish, and both white and black crappies have a preference for live minnows.

While most fishermen utilize live minnows fished from canepoles, others have found that small spinners and jigs produce adequate catches.

To differentiate between the two types of crappies, the accepted method is to count the spines on the dorsal fin: six for the white and seven or eight for the black crappie. Also, the dorsal fin is set farther forward on the white crappie.

Though popular with fishermen, the fighting ability of these fish is often belittled. True, they are quite sluggish when brought from summertime water, but a spring or winter crappie of two to three pounds will offer a fight to almost any angler. And anyone who has ever witnessed a "crappie attack" on a Tennessee T.V.A. Lake will confirm the potential of these fish.

The best months to fish for crappies are April, May and June, when the fish are spawning, and again in the early autumn until mid-December. This, of course, depends on the weather.

While spawning, crappies tend to congregate around willows in water two to three feet deep where they make their beds. About mid-June crappies retreat to deep water (twenty to twenty-five feet) and swim into shallow water only during the early morning and late, late afternoon hours. Like bream, crappies are school fish.

When crappies retreat to deep water, they can be found in deep holes conjested with stumps. By the first of autumn they again move into shallow waters and can be located in the same areas in which they spawned during the spring.

Crappies can be taken even in the dead of winter in deep water, but most of the time adverse conditions discourage this type of fishing.

A spinner tipped with porkrind is an excellent crappie seducer, as is a jig fly cast to a stump, then brought back to the surface in yo-yo fashion.

We find argument as to the eating merits of a crappie, and again it must be said that the flavor of a summer-caught crappie, like its fighting worth, is quite bland. But a spring or autumn or winter crappie is of excellent table fare and one cannot offer enough praise.

CRAPPIE-STUFFED BELL PEPPERS

(Other freshwater fish or canned tuna may be substituted for crappie.)

2 whole cleaned, medium-size crappies
2 cups water
1 t. salt
1 t. pepper
1 t. lemon juice

Place fish and remaining ingredients into pot; cover, bring to boil, reduce to simmer and cook until meat flakes when tested with fork. Remove fish to platter, cool and flake meat from bones.

Stuffing:

> 6 medium bell peppers, tops removed and seeded
> ½ cup cooked rice
> ½ cup ketchup
> 1 No. 303 can tomatoes
> ½ cup onion cooked in 1 T. vegetable oil
> Dash Worcestershire sauce

Blanch bell peppers. In mixing bowl, combine flaked fish meat, rice, ketchup, Worcestershire and onion. Fold gently and stuff peppers. Place in casserole dish and top each pepper with a tomato. Pour juice from tomatoes into bottom of dish. Place in preheated 350 degree oven for 30 minutes. Spoon pan juice over peppers every 15 minutes. Serves 6.

BROILED CRAPPIE WITH SWEET-AND-SOUR DRESSING

> 4 whole cleaned crappies
> 1 cup bottled sweet-and-sour dressing
> Salt and pepper to taste

Marinate crappies in sweet-and-sour dressing for 1 hour. Remove, salt and pepper, and place on broiler pan 4 inches from coils. Broil 8 to 10 minutes per side. Serves 4. Garnish with fresh orange slices when served on platter.

CRAPPIE PATTIES

> Flaked meat from 2 whole cooked crappies [See Crappie-Stuff-
>   ed Bell Peppers for preparing flaked crappie.]
> 1 medium onion, finely chopped
> 1 can condensed mushroom soup
> 2 eggs
> 20 saltine crackers, finely crushed
> Cracker meal as required

Combine flaked fish, onion, soup and eggs in mixing bowl. Add crushed crackers, a spoonful at a time, until mixture is workable. Shape into individual patties (2 per person), dust with cracker meal and fry in vegetable oil 4 to 5 minutes per side. Serves 4.

BAKED CRAPPIE

4 whole cleaned crappies
1 medium bell pepper, chopped
1 medium onion, chopped
1 garlic clove, chopped
2 T. vegetable oil
¼ cup melted margarine or butter

Cook pepper, onion and garlic in vegetable oil until tender. Remove and stuff into stomach cavities of crappies. Salt and pepper fish to taste, brush with melted margarine and place in lightly greased baking pan. Bake at 350 degrees, 5 minutes per pound, or until fish flakes when tested with fork. Serves 4.

CRAPPIE MARINATED IN WINE

4 whole cleaned crappies
¼ cup white wine
1 spring onion, chopped [including green top]
¼ cup melted margarine or butter
Salt and pepper to taste

Marinate fish in wine for 15 minutes. Remove fish and place in pan. Pour wine in pan and add chopped onion. Stir wine and onion together. Baste fish with melted margarine; salt and pepper and place 4 inches from coils. Broil 5 minutes per pound each side. Baste with pan juices as fish cook. Serves 4.

WHITE BASS

The white bass is widely known for its quick hits and energetic runs. And because of trading programs among state fisheries, it has become numerous in the major southern reservoirs.

Like the striped bass, white bass are schooling fish, and upon their rising to the surface, the gathering of speedboat fishermen becomes frantic. Oftentimes a limit can be hauled from a school before it sounds or returns to the depths.

The popularity of white bass lies in the fact that little study or time is required to learn how fish for them: A school "boils" the surface, you get within casting range and cast. When the lure is "smashed" you reel 'em in.

White bass are usually cooperative and this increases the angler's pleasure. For the most part, the fisherman knows that when the lure plunks a white bass will attack. But they, like all fish, are not without mood and sometimes nothing suits their pleasure. But if we were approaching a school of white bass, we would place money on making a sizable catch.

These fish, like most schooling fish, greet the new day schooling and school again at day's end. Cloudy days can sometimes produce continuous feeding.

When schooling they are vulnerable to almost any lure: small spoons, wobbling lures, spinners and small topwater plugs designed for striped bass. But for some strange reason, we have never caught a white bass on a live minnow. And we have made several fruitless attempts by casting minnows into a school.

The white bass is a good eating fish with firm texture. At dinner's end we usually leave a platter of bones with the thought that we have eaten either a small striped bass or a crappie. The taste is superb.

WHITE BASS STICKS

Slice 2 white bass fillets diagonally into widths no less than ½ inch. Salt and pepper. Dust with corn or cracker meal or flour and fry 3 to 5 minutes per side.

SPICY WHITE BASS FILLETS

4 fillets, salt and peppered to taste
¼ cup chili sauce
1 t. prepared mustard
½ t. powdered horseradish
Dash Tabasco sauce

Combine ingredients in mixing bowl and brush on fillets. Place fish on broiler pan 4 inches from coils and broil 5 to 8 minutes per side. Baste with mixture again when fillets are turned. Serves 4.

CREAMED WHITE BASS WITH HAM

(Ham is preferred but baked chicken or turkey — skin removed — may be substituted.)

1 whole cleaned white bass
1 cup diced ham
1 cup water
1 t. salt
1 t. lemon juice
1 can condensed mushroom soup
1 soup can sweet milk
½ T. pimiento, chopped

Place fish in pot with water, salt, lemon juice. Cover, bring to a boil; reduce heat to simmer and cook until meat flakes when tested with fork (about 10 minutes.) Remove fish from pot and, when cooled, flake or separate into small chunks. Into saucepan, empty condensed soup and milk and heat slowly. When just before bubbling, add ham, chicken or turkey and fish and pimiento. Stir gently until hot. Serve over toast or pastry shells to 4 to 6 people. (A dash of cooking sherry enhances the flavor.)

BROILED WHITE BASS

4 fillets
¼ cup melted margarine or butter
8 to 10 celery tops
2 whole thin-sliced lemons
Juice of 1 lemon
Salt and pepper to taste

In shallow glass casserole dish, make bed of celery tops and sliced lemons. Baste both sides of fillets with melted margarine; salt and pepper fish and place on celery-lemon bed. Pour lemon juice over fish, place 4 inches from coils and broil 5 to 8 minutes per side. Serves 4.

JACKFISH

We do not know the precise hour because we did not have a watch. Maybe it was 10 a.m. or maybe it was 11 or 11:30. We don't know that it really makes much difference. Whatever the hour, the fish were rolling and slashing the water as if they had been on a hunger strike.

There are only two settings one adheres to while fishing: sunrise and sunset. You enter at sunrise and leave at sunset. A watch does nothing more than remind you of where you should or shouldn't be, what you've got to do or didn't do and how much time you've got to do it in. Once or twice we have emerged from fishing not at sunset but at sunrise on the second day. But that's another story and a watch would not have solved or avoided that predicament.

We tossed a black- and yellow-tailed spinner bait between the slingshot prong of a partially submerged tree. We'd made maybe three or four cranks on the bait-casting reel when the spool curls on the line snapped to attention.

The rod tip went into convulsions and a mist of spray water-hosed from the spool as we pressed our thumb against the spool to break the speed of the line and spirit of the fish. The fish whirlpooled the water several times and cleared the surface. A jackfish! Lord, what a jackfish — maybe three pounds — and his head pitched like an angry bull's.

The spinner bait's hook and the black-and-yellow skirt were hanging from his lower jaw. And we could see the long, needlepointed teeth—row after row of them—as we slipped the dip net under him.

Jackfish or pike, as they are called in the South, belong to the pickerel family. Much like catfish, they have had poor public relations and are considered by many to be villains. They can steal a minnow quicker than any fish, snap a line as if it were sewing thread and dismantle a pole hemmed in a willow thicket. But there are positive requisites to be considered. They are truly magnificent leapers and they will hit just about any type of plug. Their favorite food is the live minnow.

Jackfish favor the same cover as largemouth bass — heavy brush areas, log- and stump-infested waters, weedbeds and dense lily growths.

Most anglers who fish for jackfish use a wire leader to prevent the saw-tooth mouth from severing the line. A jackfish seems to prefer a fast target and anglers who fish topwater or underwater plugs very fast seem to get best results.

The meat of a jackfish is extremely sweet, but the jack's bony structure does present somewhat of a problem. However, the flavorful meat is sufficient reward for those who sit and separate meat from bones.

JACKFISH BUTTERFLY FILLETS

Salt and pepper jackfish fillets. Dust with corn meal and fry in vegetable oil 3 to 5 minutes per side.

Variation:

Baste with fresh lemon juice, salt and pepper. Broil 4 inches from coils, 5 to 8 minutes per side. One butterfly fillet per person. (See Cleaning and Freezing Fish for preparation of a butterfly fillet.)

BROILED JACKFISH WITH TOMATO SAUCE

2 butterfly fillets [refer to Cleaning and Freezing Fish for preparation]
¼ cup melted margarine or butter

Salt and pepper fillets to taste; brush with melted margarine and broil 4 inches from coils, 5 to 8 minutes per side.

Tomato Sauce

While fillets are broiling, prepare in saucepan:

1 small can tomato sauce
½ T. melted margarine or butter
1 t. salt
½ t. black pepper
Dash Worcestershire sauce

Cook on medium heat and pour over broiled fillets when removed from oven to platter.

(If, by chance, you happen to have a tablespoon or two of chicken gravy, add to the above ingredients. It adds body and flavor to the tomato sauce.)

JACK PARMESAN

1 whole cleaned jackfish, 1½ lbs. upward
½ cup sour cream
¼ cup melted margarine or butter
½ cup grated Parmesan cheese

In mixing bowl combine sour cream, margarine and cheese. Spread sauce over salt-and-peppered fish in baking pan. Bake at 350 degrees, 5 minutes per pound each side, or until mixture is brown and fish flakes when tested with fork. Serves 4.

BAKED JACK WITH HERBS

1 whole cleaned jack, 1½ lbs. upward
¼ cup melted margarine or butter
¼ T. parsley flakes
¼ T. prepared herb seasoning
¼ t. oregano
½ t. dill weed

Combine ingredients in mixing bowl and baste fish inside and out. Place in baking pan and into 350 degree oven and bake 5 minutes per pound per side. Serves 4.

TROUT

The brook trout is a native of the Southeast's mountain wilds, but the brown and rainbow trout are imports. The brown is of European origin and the rainbow is from the Pacific coast. They are truly beautiful fish and add greatly to our coldwater streams and the surrounding flora and fauna.

Long before the brown and rainbow trout were introduced to our mountain streams, the brook trout was the fisherman's fish: a savage striker and none too particular at feeding time. But the brook

trout has never tolerated civilization. Today, for the most part, this trout—at least that not of hatchery origin—is isolated in the uppermost mountain streams and pools where only the hardiest of fishermen venture.

If it were not for put-and-take trout programs, there would be little, if any, trout fishing in the Southeast. Each year, literally hundreds of thousands of trout are dumped into mountain streams, and they are greeted by as many fishermen—from barefoot boys armed with canepoles to the most dedicated of fly fishermen.

While most of these catchable-sized trout are caught almost immediately upon release, some escape and reach an admirable size. It is not common, but one occasionally hears word of a five-pound rainbow or brown being hooked.

No purist fly fisherman would be without a Royal Coachman, a Parmachene Belle, or a brown or gray hackle. While the fly fishermen's commitment is admired, the truth is that most of these put-and-take trout are caught on canned corn, earthworms or crickets—especially the rainbow. Small spoons and spinners are also favored for the rainbow, brown and brook trout.

We must relate our first trout expedition to Arkansas's White River where there is excellent rainbow trout fishing.

We had devoured a hefty diet of trout fishing techniques and upon arrival were prepared mentally and attired in the finest of trout fishing regalia. Yet, we fished and caught nothing until we met an old mountain man who promptly taught us secrets of the rainbow. We took our first White River rainbow on a healthy redworm dug from a nearby pasture.

The trout has long been the delight of the epicure as well as the sportsman, as the following recipes will prove.

BAKED TROUT WITH WINE-ALMOND SAUCE

4 ½- to 1-lb. whole cleaned trout
¼ cup melted margarine or butter

Salt and pepper trout; brush with melted margarine, place in pan and bake 5 minutes per pound per side.

Wine-Almond Sauce

1 cup almonds
½ cup melted margarine or butter
½ cup white wine
1 cup water

Blanch almonds quickly in boiling water. Remove, peel and either shave or chop fine. Melt margarine or butter in saucepan. Add almonds and brown. Blend with wine and pour over baked trout on serving platter. Serves 4.

BROILED TROUT WITH MUSHROOMS

4 ½- to 1-lb. whole cleaned trout
¼ cup melted margarine or butter
Salt and pepper to taste
1 T. margarine or butter
1 2-oz. can mushroom stems and pieces

Brush trout with melted margarine (¼ cup); salt and pepper. Place on broiler pan and broil 4 inches from coils, 5 minutes per pound per side. While trout are cooking, in saucepan add 1 tablespoon margarine and heat. When melted, add mushrooms (reserve liquid) and cook on medium heat until mushrooms brown. When browned, add mushroom liquid and heat. When trout are done, remove to platter and spoon mushrooms and sauce over fish. Serves 4.

SKILLET-FRIED TROUT

4 ½- to 1-lb. whole cleaned trout
¼ cup vegetable oil or shortening
½ cup cracker or corn meal

Salt and pepper trout to taste. Dust with corn meal. At high temperature, heat oil to bubbling; place trout in oil, reduce to medium and fry 3 to 5 minutes per side. Serves 4.

SHAD ROE

It is to the sport fisherman's delight that shad—either the American or hickory shad and not to be confused with the gizzard shad, a baitfish eaten only by other fish—are of exceptional fighting quality.

Our first shad fishing expedition occured in the Savannah River—a river shared by South Carolina and Georgia—some years ago, and we have long remembered the gusto with which a shad tackles a small wobbling spoon. Their hit and drive, coupled with many surface leaps, reminds us of a tarpon, and they are fondly called "freshwater tarpon" by many fishermen.

Like the rockfish chapter, this chapter on shad could easily have been placed in the saltwater section. Both are of saltwater origin and, except for landlocked stripers, enter coastal tributaries only to spawn.

Shad, like most fish, are influenced by water temperature and the moon when it comes time to spawn. A 50-degree water temperature and full moon in February signal their migration. By mid-April, spawning accomplished, they return to the ocean. Very little is known of their habits or whereabouts after they reenter saltwater.

A light-action spinning rod with no more than six-pound line is quite adequate to handle shad. Jig flies and small spoons are favored by many fishermen. A flyrod is an excellent rod to use.

By no means does a shad run indicate success for a game fisherman. These fish are finicky while spawning and the angler will often bring in nothing. It is generally accepted that shad do not eat while spawning; why they are sometimes attracted to artificial bait is not known. But we consider their unpredictable mood as a sporting plus since the angler must be willing to match wits with them.

North Carolina's Cape Fear River is highly regarded for its shad, as is Florida's St. John's River. Georgia also has several rivers of repute. South Carolina's Waccamaw and Pee Dee rivers realize a commercial catch of over 71,000 pounds annually, while the Edisto River yields some 17,000 pounds. The Edisto, like the Savannah, is highly favored by sport fishermen.

Shad roe is one of the most widely known commercially processed fish eggs. However, roe from crappies, largemouths, bream and redbreasts, to name only a few, is also flavorsome.

FRIED SHAD ROE IN BACON DRIPPINGS

2 sets roe [1 set per person]
4 slices breakfast bacon
¼ cup craker or corn meal

Place roe in saucepan; barely cover with water and place over medium heat. Cover saucepan and cook 5 to 8 minutes. While roe is cooking, fry bacon in skillet. When done, remove bacon and leave fat in skillet. Gently remove roe from pot; salt and pepper and dust lightly with cracker meal. Reheat bacon fat on medium heat, add roe and fry 4 to 5 minutes, constantly turning roe in pan. Remove to platter and garnish with bacon. Serves 2.

BROILED SHAD ROE

2 sets roe
¼ cup melted margarine or butter

Prepare Fried Roe as above. Remove roe from saucepan and baste with melted margarine; salt and pepper. Place on broiler pan 4 inches from coils and broil 6 to 8 minutes. Serves 2.

SAUTÉED SHAD ROE

2 sets roe
¼ cup margarine or butter
1 T. lemon or lime juice
1/8 t. oregano

Place roe in saucepan; barely cover with water and place over medium heat. Cover saucepan and cook 5 to 8 minutes.

Melt margarine or butter in skillet on medium heat; add lemon or lime juice and oregano. Blend, add parboiled roe and cook (constantly turning, bringing juices over roe) for 6 to 7 minutes. Remove, place on serving platter and pour pan drippings over roe.

Part II

Saltwater Fish

DOLPHIN

The Gulf Stream is a warm ocean current flowing out from the Gulf of Mexico northward to Nantucket Island, where it is deflected eastward across the Atlantic Ocean. The water, depending on the height of the sun and its angle or reflection, is either a cooling deep blue or a lime green when the ocean winds ripple the surface.

The Stream is the curator of a vast assortment of fish and marine life and it is here that dolphins jerk lines free from long-armed outriggers. The sound of the line leaving the outrigger is similar to the firing of a small-bore rifle.

Gulf Stream dolphins are bathed in a rainbow of colors, but this beauty if only skin deep. Beneath beats the heart of a fighter. Incredibly swift, a dolphin, while in pursuit of his prey, will often charge from many yards away, then vault from the water and crash down upon its victim. When hooked, he is even more dynamic: He will make a smoking run, leaping into the air time after time. Even when near exhaustion, his weakest effort may equal the strongest of another fish.

Dolphins usually run in schools and when one is hooked the angler can make ready for another since they have a curious habit of playing follow the leader.

Dolphins seem to favor floating objects and drifting weed lines. The bigger the object the more dolphins that will be attracted, as a rule. They need little coaxing to strike. The practiced method for a charter boat skipper is to troll and cover a wide range of territory for the paying clientele.

Since most schooling dolphins seldom weigh over six pounds, light tackle can be used with success. A spinning rod with ten-pound test line is quite adequate, but because of the dolphins' jetlike runs, reels should have a minimum of two hundred yards of line. Feathered jigs and wobbling spoons work quite well.

Schooling dolphins, like schooling largemouths, are very spirited, but they are naive also and show little concern for danger. Their eager attempts to outrun, outcatch and outfight a big bull dolphin usually proves fatal when hooked.

Leaps become frantic and, since they are young and not conditioned to the fight, their punches are too fast. Undisciplined energy is consumed within minutes. Beaten, they roll to the surface and flounder until the gaff finds its mark.

The old bulls, speed and agility diminished by time, move with caution, lead the fight and employ both muscle and wisdom. Such logic does not seem possible for a fish, but we have seen a bull dolphin strip the bait from around the hook, leaving only cold, white flashing steel in the Stream.

A blue marlin can do this with some finesse, but not like an old bull dolphin. However, we have encountered more bull dolphins than blue marlins and the last blue marlin cured us of ever wanting to fight another.

For eating purposes, young dolphins are the best because they are small and the meat has not had time to become thick, grainy and bland.

MEDITERRANEAN-FRIED DOLPHIN

2 lbs. fillets sliced in individual servings
¼ cup wine vinegar
1/8 t. cayenne
¼ cup olive oil
1 small onion, chopped
1/8 t. garlic, minced
½ t. thyme

Combine ingredients in bowl, pour over fillets and marinate for 30 minutes. Remove, dust with cracker or corn meal and fry in preheated oil 3 to 5 minutes per side. Serves 6.

DOLPHIN NEWBURG

¼ lb. dolphin fillet [makes 1 cup flaked meat]
1½ cups water
1 t. salt
½ t. black pepper
1 T. lemon juice
1 bay leaf, crumbled

Place water, salt, pepper, lemon juice and bay leaf into pot; cover, bring to boil, reduce to simmer for 10 minutes to activate seasonings. Place dolphin into pot, bring back to boil, reduce to simmer and cook 10 to 12 minutes or until meat begins to flake. Remove meat, cool, then flake. If meat measures more than 1 cup, place excess in container and freeze for further use.

Under Sauces to Accompany Fish, see Newburg Sauce. Make sauce, add flaked dolphin, blend and serve either on toast points or pastry shells to 4.

BROILED DOLPHIN WITH GREEN TOMATOES

Fillets for 4 persons
¼ cup melted margarine or butter

Tomato Marinade

1 large green tomato
1 T. olive oil
1 garlic clove, finely chopped

Slice tomato and place in small bowl. Add olive oil and garlic. Marinate for 15 minutes. Remove tomato slices from marinade and set aside.

Brush fillets with margarine, salt and pepper. Place on broiler pan 4 inches from coils. Broil 5 to 8 minutes per side. When fillets are turned, let cook until just before browning and place marinated tomatoes on top of fillets. Allow tomatoes to brown before serving fish.

OUR FAVORITE BROILED DOLPHIN

4 fillets marinated in 1 cup lime juice for 1 hour
1 No. 303 can tomatoes
1 large onion, thinly sliced
2 fresh limes, sliced
¼ cup melted margarine or butter

Remove fish from marinade; salt and pepper to taste and brush with margarine. Place on broiler pan and cook 4 inches from coils, 5 to 8 minutes per side. Turn, brush with margarine, salt and pepper, and top with onions, limes and tomatoes and complete broiling. Serve to 4.

SHEEPSHEAD

To catch a sheepshead you must have the patience and the stubbornness of a mule. You literally have to set the hook before he strikes. There are few fish as cantankerous as this one.

Countless sheepshead have been caught from beneath oceanside docks, bridge pilings and reefs. Light to medium tackle is used for sheepshead fishing and this includes canepoles, casting rods, spinning rods and flyrods. Even the handline is effective.

Although some artificial lures such as jigs can be used, the dedicated sheepshead angler uses fiddler crabs—the classic sheepshead bait. Any low-tide marsh will yield all the fiddler crabs desired.

Find a bridge piling, bait up with a lively fiddler and begin fishing. A strong crappie hook can be used, but forget about using those skinny wire hooks. A big sheepshead will gnaw through it as though it were sewing thread.

To entice them further you can mince mullet, shrimp and clams into a chum and scatter it around the area you intend to fish.

While you do have a wide selection of rods to choose from, the best outfit would be one sensitive enough to telegraph the touch of a sheepshead feeding on a dangling fiddler crab. The line must be held if you are to feel the mouselike snipping below. Otherwise, the fish will remove all your bait.

How big do sheepshead get? Well, a three to four pounder is considered a good fish, but we've heard of fifteen and twenty pounders.

The sheepshead is a sturdy, grinding battler; his nickname—"goathead"—does not derive from gentleness at rod's end. We dare say that if a sheepshead were a jumping fish, he would be classed in sporting circles with the dolphin or the bluefish.

Lord, we love to catch sheepshead, fillet them, cook them till the flesh turns golden under a broiler, and the butter and lime juice sauce oozes from their flesh and drips and pops on a hot broiler pan.

BROILED SHEEPSHEAD

4 fillets
¼ cup melted margarine or butter combined with 2 T. lime juice
Paprika

Salt and pepper fillets to taste. Baste with margarine-lime mixture; broil 4 inches from coils, 5 to 8 minutes each side. Remove to platter, sprinkle with paprika, garnish with fresh parsley sprigs and serve to 4.

PAN-FRIED SHEEPSHEAD

4 ½- to ¾-lb. whole cleaned sheepshead
½ cup vegetable oil
½ cup cracker or corn meal

Salt and pepper to taste. Dust with meal. Heat oil to bubbling on high heat. Enter fish, reduce heat to medium and fry 3 to 5 minutes per side. Serve to 4.

SHEEPSHEAD IN WINE

4 fillets
¼ cup white wine

Salt and pepper fillets; place in lightly oiled, shallow baking pan or oven-proof dish. Add wine and cook 5 minutes per pound (or until fish flakes easily when tested with fork) in 350 degree oven. Garnish with spring onions and serve to 4.

BLUEFISH

They came in great amphibious waves—uninhibited savages of the seas, chopping, slashing as they bulldogged their blue bodies through the surf at North Carolina's Outer Banks near the village of Buxton. The refuse left by feeding bluefish spilled onto the beach.

The wind blew from every direction and with each gust the waves curled, dropped and bathed us in brine. And the cold—the cold was as we have never known. The feet of our waders filled with water, our eyes burned from the salt and our arms ached with each savage run of a blue. Beyond the breakers the fish churned and tainted the water red from each new kill. The wind gathered loose beach sand and spit it at those who stood belt-deep in water and fought the unyielding blues.

Gulls, feathers fluffed against the cold and wind, ate the refuse washed ashore by the feeding fish with bodies of sparkling blue—fish endowed with beauty, and fortitude to fight against the hook and surf angler's long rod and strength.

The blues had been in the surf since daylight and they would remain until dark—perhaps all night.

The surf on the Outer Banks is infamous for its brutality. The current, engaged in immortal conflict, crushes each wave and disperses it into a white salty mist. Bluefish, in harmony with the violent reaction of currents and tide, gather here in vast schools.

The strike and fight of the bluefish is of even greater distinction than that of the channel bass or the striped bass. They are not as large as the latter fish, but their bodies are compact, designed for ultimate speed, and we insist that their strike is more one of sadistic pleasure than one of hunger satisfaction.

A blue hits with a ricochet effect and immediately streaks to where the water is most turbulent. Once inside the turbulence, he will roll, jump, twist, turn and bulldog. A wire leader on the line is a must.

The typical weight of blues, two to four pounds, is somewhat misleading as they may reach fifteen pounds and larger. On the Outer Banks where the gulls and blues came together, long surf rods strained with bluefish of twelve and fifteen pounds.

When fishing for blues, the rod should be sturdy, but not hickory tough, the leader a No. 2, the line at least two hundred yards and hook from a 3/0 to a 7/0 in size.

The relentless drive of bluefish toward their prey renders them incapable of choice. They will smash a cut-mullet rig fished on the bottom as quickly as they will seize a flashing spoon.

We had long since tired of standing near-frozen in the icy surf and being battered by volleys of waves. Our back revolted with seizures of pain as we stood quivering in the water, and the thought of another fight was fading as rapidly as was the day. A pink hue embraced the Outer Banks as flocks of wildfowl gathered for sleep. The passion with which we had attacked the blues had dissipated into a warm feeling in inward satisfaction. We had seen bluefish in the surf as we had longed to do, had hung, caught and lost an appreciable number.

Although listed among the top fighters of the sea, bluefish are not without fault: Their flesh is oily, soft and suitable only for frying and broiling. Even frying and broiling have limitations. Bluefish upwards of two and two and a half pounds are excellent when fried or broiled. Larger fish must be broiled.

Also, bluefish should be cooked within twenty-four hours of capture and the dark flesh, which will become mushy if not removed, should be discarded. If not prepared within this period the texture of the fish will deteriorate and become bitter.

Freezing? We have unsuccessfully tried to freeze bluefish. The flesh and taste seem to deteriorate during the process. But we can overlook some of their cooking and preservation limitations for just one bluefish properly prepared.

LEMON-AND-PEPPER BLUEFISH

4 fillets
1 T. prepared lemon-and-pepper seasoning
Juice of 3 lemons
Salt and pepper

Mix prepared lemon-and-pepper seasoning with lemon juice. Pour over fish in bowl, cover with plastic wrap and refrigerate for 3 hours. Remove, salt and pepper and broil 4 inches from coils, 5 to 8 minutes per side. Baste with lemon juice and lemon-and-pepper seasoning marinade. Serve to 4.

BROILED BLUEFISH

2 lbs. bluefish fillets
¼ cup melted shortening or vegetable oil
2 T. lemon juice
1 t. salt
1 t. black pepper

Cut fish into serving-size portions. Combine oil, lemon juice, salt and pepper. Place fish on lightly greased broiler pan and baste with seasoned oil. Broil 4 inches from coils, 5 to 8 minutes per side. Serves 6.

PAN-FRIED BLUEFISH

4 whole, bluefish, cleaned 1 to 1½ pounds each
2 t. salt
1 t. black pepper
1 t. prepared herb seasoning
1 t. garlic salt
½ cup vegetable oil

Mix salt, pepper, herb seasoning and garlic salt together. Season fish and dust lightly with cracker or corn meal. Heat vegetable oil to bubbling on high heat; enter fish, reduce to medium and fry 3 to 5 minutes per side. Serve to 4.

RED SNAPPER

The red snapper is a deep, deep water fish and home is the Gulf Stream or close-by. This is a party boat fisherman's fish, and almost any morning—early, early morning—you can go down to the dock, pay a small fee, board a party boat (better known as a head boat) and fish the "snapper banks." No equipment need be furnished by you and no angling experience is required. Since a rather large number of fishermen, many of which are tourists, do seek these fish, one can apply the term, "sportfishing." But for the most part, red snapper enter into the commerical fishing category.

There is absolutely no sport—fighting sport—in catching a red snapper. This is not to degrade those who find pleasure in snapper fishing; there is just no challenge in pitting oneself against the fish.

If the weather holds, and this is a mighty big "if" when dealing with the ocean, you arrive at the fishing grounds, where heavily weighted, baited lines are cast overboard and go down...down... down. If the fish are there, you can sometimes reel up two or three fish at once.

Those aboard the party boat who use hand-cranked reels are to be congratulated on their physical strength. However, for the less physical, there are electric reels aboard; when the snapper bites, you push a button and up comes the fish.

Party fishermen must be congratulated on their ability to rise before man was meant to rise and their willingness to brave a slow, rocking, bouncing, knocking trip to the snapper banks. While we are not listed in either the strong or the brave category, we have enjoyed some rather fruitful and sometimes hilarious adventures en route to and from the snapper banks.

If you've been, then you know of what we write. If not, then you must go and learn.

Oftentime an individual's snapper catch will more than pay for his trip when sold back at dockside. The red snapper is one of the best-known saltwater fish and its superb taste is renowned—especially when prepared with a stuffing.

RED SNAPPER WITH SHRIMP STUFFING

1 4- to 5-lb. whole cleaned snapper
2 T. melted margarine or butter
1 T. Worcestershire sauce
Salt and pepper

Beginning at base of gill, cut fish down stomach to thick part of tail. Fill with shrimp stuffing (See Breads and Stuffings.) Place in baking pan with 1 cup water. Salt and pepper. Combine margarine with Worestershire and baste fish. Place pan into 350 degree oven and bake 5 minutes per pound each side. Serves 4 to 6.

BROILED RED SNAPPER FILLETS

2 lbs. red snapper fillets, cut into serving portions
1 t. salt
½ t. black pepper
1 t. paprika
2 T. lime juice
1 t. onion, grated
½ cup melted margarine or butter

Combine ingredients. Place fish on broiler pan; baste and broil 4 inches from coils, 5 to 8 minutes per side. Serves 6.

ANOTHER BAKED RED SNAPPER

1 3- to 4-lb. whole cleaned snapper

In bowl mix:

1 small can tomato sauce
1 t. salt
½ t. black pepper
1 T. lemon juice
1/8 t. cayenne pepper
¼ cup bell pepper, chopped

Combine ingredients. Place fish in baking pan and pour mixture over fish. Bake at 350 degrees, 5 minutes per pound. Serve to 4.

CHANNEL BASS

The strike of a channel bass (drum or spottail if you prefer) is not vicious, but gentle. Here is a fish who likes to smell, taste and sample—a nudger. Only when the striking fish begins to machine gun the rod tip do you take up slack line and force the hook to penetrate with one swift and very hard yank.

To strike while the fish is teasing the bait is to lose the fish. You must give him time to work the bait to the rear of his throat. The only exception to this occurs when fishing with spoons; the retrieve and strike combined will set the hook.

On the South Carolina coast, most channel bass fishing is done with bait such as cut mullet, shrimp and squid. Northward, artificials seem to take favor over bait fishing. We have taken several on large saltwater spoons, but never one over ten pounds. It is explosive and stimulating to take a hit with a spoon. Yet it's more relaxing to stand in the surf and let your bait do the bidding.

The season for channel bass fishermen is limited. They fish during the spring and autumn runs, on the incoming and outgoing tides. The tide is the "dinner bell" for ocean fish as it brings and recalls food. This may be an oversimplification of the sport, but it's the basis of the game.

For the most part, channel bass fishing is a process of fishing the right tide during a run and keeping the bait in the water.

Unlike other ocean species, channel bass seldom congregate in great schools where they herd schools of baitfish and charge. Although the surf may be thick with the bottom-foraging channel bass, visual signs of their feeding along the beach are rare to the fisherman.

With the exception of points or inlets (where sloughs may not be present), most channel bass fishing is done in sloughs along the beach. This is nothing more than an avenue or hole created by the surf and tides between the beach and outer bar. These fish usually prefer a slough with one or more escape routes to the ocean. Long stretches of unbroken bar are not favorable and seldom will the angler locate fish here. Those areas where you can wade and fish the entrances, easily located at low tide, are fruitful when channel bass enter these passages to feed.

Few bass are taken when the water has been clouded by high winds—and even fewer on calm days. Winds of ten to fifteen knots are the most productive as they agitate the surf and uncover clams and marine worms on which the bass feed.

One cannot overemphasize how finicky channel bass are. While you may connect with three, four or more on a day when the wind, tide, surf and fish have all collaborated in your favor, there is a chance you may get one and only one strike.

You must make the strike count. The hook or hooks should be razor sharp, the reel in mint condition and the line free of weak spots.

After the bait (if you're fishing fresh mullet) has entered the surf, reel in just enough line to keep a little tension, but not enough to let the fish sense a fixed object. A tight line will result in the fishes' releasing the bait as he picks it up and begins to move. Set the drag until you think it will check the run, but not to the breaking point. If the fish if of such size that more drag need be applied, do so after the hook is planted and the fish is on a straightaway course.

Channel bass, and this is a personal preference, are succulent from a half pound up to ten and twelve pounds. For larger fish the meat is coarse and void of the delicate taste so desired in fish cookery.

WHOLE PAN-FRIED BASS

4 1- to 1½-lb. whole cleaned bass
½ cup vegetable oil
1 t. salt
½ t. black pepper
½ t. oregano
1/8 t. cayenne
Cracker or corn meal

Mix salt, pepper, oregano and cayenne in dish. Season fish and dust with meal. Bring oil to bubbling on high heat; enter fish, reduce to medium heat and fry 3 to 5 minutes per side. Serves 4.

BAKED BASS WITH MUSHROOM-RICE STUFFING

1 4- to 5-lb. whole cleaned bass
¼ cup margarine or butter

Salt and pepper fish and baste with melted margarine or butter. Stuff stomach cavity with mushroom-rice stuffing (see Breads and Stuffings) and place in baking pan with 1 cup water. Bake at 350 degrees, 5 minutes per pound each side. Serves 4 to 6.

BASS FILLETS WITH CHEESE SAUCE

1 lb. fillets cut in serving portions
¼ cup melted butter or margarine

Salt and pepper fillets to taste; baste with margarine, place on broiler pan and broil 4 inches from coils 5 to 8 minutes per side. Remove broiled fillets to serving platter and ladle with Cheese Sauce. (See Sauces to Accompany Fish.) Serves 4.

SPANISH AND KING MACKEREL

The Spanish and king mackerels are both highly sought for their battling antics, and when one thinks of going either for the Spanish or the king, the mind conjurs a glass-slipper ocean with jumping bait fish and mackerels cutting and thinning their ranks. Though the king mackerel may be larger, the Spanish mackerel yields nothing to his size. The Spanish mackerel is perhaps the scrappiest of all ocean fish and, with its irridescence and spots, one of the most colorful.

The battling reputation these fish have gained is not rumor but fact. Extremely swift, a hooked Spanish mackerel will zip to the surface with a combination of jumps and leaps. Upon returning to the water, he will maintain a barrage of leaps, jumps, dives and darts until he is either free or subdued.

Medium-action rods with twelve-pound test line will suffice. Flashing spoons either cast into feeding schools or trolled and fished fast will produce.

A wire leader is a must to keep mackerels from cutting themselves loose. If a school is large and thick, the line may be cut above the leader by an open-mouthed Spanish mackerel chasing bait fish. A hook of 6/0 to 8/0 should be used.

The king mackerel, like the Spanish, is a school fish and there are times when acre upon acre of feeding kings can be seen. The action is quick, heart pounding and tedious after the sixth or seventh king is brought aboard.

Both South and North Carolina are noted for their king mackerel runs, and coastal anglers in each of the Carolinas are quick to point out that "their" waters harbor more kings.

Unlike the Spanish mackerel, the king enjoys an underwater battle more than a surface exhibition. But this is not to say a king won't jump. He is quite capable of high hurdles; when he decides to surface, his leaps are nothing short of spectacular.

Sporting though they are, the value of these two fish is not fully understood until they are prepared for eating.

SPANISH MACKEREL WITH LEMON-CHIVE SAUCE

4 fillets
¼ cup melted margarine or butter

Salt and pepper fillets; baste with margarine, place on broiler pan and broil 4 inches from coils, 5 to 8 minutes per side. Prepare Lemon-Chive Sauce. (See Sauces to Accompany Fish.) Remove fillets to serving platter and ladle with sauce. Serve to 4.

TANGY BROILED MACKEREL

4 whole fillets
¼ cup lemon juice
¼ cup French dressing, bottled
1 t. salt
½ t. black pepper

Combine ingredients and marinate fish 15 minutes. Remove fish, place on broiler pan and cook 4 inches from coils, 5 to 8 minutes per side. Serve to 4.

PINEAPPLE SPANISH MACKEREL

4 fillets
¼ cup melted margarine or butter
Salt and pepper
1 cup pineapple juice
Cornstarch to thicken

Salt and pepper fillets, baste with margarine, place on broiler pan and broil 4 inches from coils, 5 to 8 minutes per side. When done, remove to heated serving platter. In saucepan, bring pineapple juice to rolling boil; thicken to medium sauce with cornstarch. Ladle over Spanish mackerel fillets and serve to 4.

FRIED KING MACKEREL STEAKS

4 mackerel steaks
Salt and pepper
Cracker or corn meal
¼ cup vegetalbe oil

Season steaks with salt, pepper and dust lightly with corn meal. Bring vegetable oil to bubbling; enter steaks, reduce to medium heat and cook 4 to 6 minutes per side. Serve to 4.

BROILED KING MACKEREL STEAKS

4 mackerel steaks
¼ cup melted margarine or butter

Salt and pepper steaks. Baste with margarine, place on broiler pan and broil 4 inches from coils, 5 to 8 minutes per side. Serve to 4. (A Vinaigrette Sauce also enhances this dish. See Flounder Vinaigrette.)

BAKED KING MACKEREL

1 3- to 4-lb. whole cleaned mackerel
¼ cup melted margarine or butter
1 t. salt
½ t. black pepper
1 t. marjoram leaves

Combine margarine, salt, pepper and marjoram leaves. Baste fish inside and out. Place fish in baking pan; add 1 cup water, bake at 350 degrees, 5 minutes per pound each side, or until fish flakes easily when tested with fork. Serve to 4.

SALTWATER TROUT

In South Carolina they are called summer or winter trout, this depending, of course, on whether it's summer or winter. Northward, anglers fondly call them speckled or sea trout. We are speaking of the weakfish, a name which does little justice to the fighting reputation of the saltwater trout.

It's not really important what you call them, for these fish are pure excitement from the time word works inland from the coast that "the trout are in!"

A rewarding characteristic of these fish is that they can be caught using several methods: trolling, still-fishing and casting with plugs, spoons and feathered jigs.

It's hard to predict where they will be from day to day, but areas such as bays, inlets, channels or creeks that have extensive underwater grass beds are all ideal trout drops.

Deep holes around shell banks are not to be overlooked, especially during a high or running tide as trout tend to concentrate in such

places during these tidal changes. But be warned that trout know well how to make use of underwater shell banks to sever lines.

While most coastal anglers use live shrimp for trout, others are dyed-in-the-wool artifical purists and the controversy between the two has no end in sight—because both catch fish.

The proper way to hook a live shrimp is to pass the hook's point just below the horn across the top of the head. Care should be taken not to penetrate the dark area of the head. Puncture the dark spot and almost instantly the shrimp will die. The idea is to keep the shrimp live and snapping.

A smooth, steady cast is important. If not, the shrimp will go in one direction and the empty rig in the other. The live-shrimp rig usually consists of twelve-pound test line, a five-inch cork, sinker and a 3/0 hook.

Once the rig hits the water, take up the slack and retrieve the cork, popping it several times during the retrieve. The popping cork is supposed to imitate shrimp jumping in the area. A trout will sometimes tug the cork down when he takes the shrimp, but the strike is usually a quick one.

Fishing with artificials requires a different approach, simply because it's an artificial bait and the angler has to make the bait come to life.

The meat of the saltwater trout is of exceptional quality as is that of the freshwater trout. It is firm, savory and especially tasty baked.

TROUT WITH WHITE WINE SAUCE

1 2- to 3-lb. whole cleaned trout
1 T. melted margarine or butter
1 t. Worcestershire sauce
1 t. prepared herb seasoning
1 t. salt
½ t. black pepper

Combine ingredients; baste trout inside and out and bake in 350 degree oven 5 minutes per pound each side. When trout is done, remove to heated platter and ladle with white wine sauce. (See Sauces to Accompany Fish for Wine Sauce.) Serves 4.

TROUT FILLETS WITH OYSTER SAUCE

4 whole fillets
¼ cup melted margarine or butter

Salt and pepper fillets, brush with margarine and broil 4 inches from coils 5 to 8 minutes per side. Ladle with Oyster Sauce. (See Sauces to Accompany fish.) Serves 4.

TROUT ORIENTAL

1 cup cooked, flaked meat
1 rib of celery, chopped
1 small onion, chopped
1 medium bell pepper, chopped
1½ cups chicken broth or 2 chicken bouillon cubes dissolved in
    2 cups hot water
1 T. Chinese [beaded] molasses
1 T. soy sauce
Cornstarch to thicken

In small pot combine ½ cup water, celery, onion and bell pepper. Cover, bring to boil, reduce to medium heat and cook until vegetables are tender, **not mushy**. When done, add chicken stock. Bring back to boil and thicken to medium sauce with cornstarch. Add molasses; stir. Add soy sauce and flaked fish. Stir and serve over steamed rice. Top with chinese noodles. Serves 4.

SHARK

We were in North Carolina's blue water, some eighty miles off-shore from Morehead City, and had spent most of the day fighting a mad ocean dominated by thirty-five knot winds.

The ocean's temper was short and we the victims. Skipper Bruce Tapscott tended the wheel, first mate Eddie Tapscott kept the lines, sportfisherman Joel Arrington offered support and Perry Jenifer and I supported one another.

Midday came and went and the crew had plucked but three bonito from the raging sea. A bitter fluid rose to my throat and stayed. Only if you have undergone such conditions can you know the feelings.

"A hit!" Eddie yelled.

The portside rod had a deep bend. A mist of saltwater spewed from the reel.

"Who wants 'im?" Eddie asked, looking around.

"You take 'im, Perry," Joel and I said in unison.

Perry occupied a fighting chair, both hands gripping the rod. Line was still leaving the spool.

This fish had yet to show his colors. The elimination process began. Dolphin? No. A dolphin would would have long since taken to the air, jumping and skittering. Wahoo? Doubtful. Wahoo, like dolphin, are great exhibitionists. King mackerel? Kings do run rather deep, yet a king also enjoys surface play.

This fish had yet to make an attempt to surface but ran deeper. The veins of Perry's strained arms were visible as was the sweat that coursed his back and chest. His lips were dry and a film of salt whitened them. I lifted a cup of water to his lips and he drank in rushing gulps.

Yellowfin tuna? There would be meat for all if this fish proved to be a yellowfin. Yes, he had hit as a yellowfin would, driving and diving deep, deeper, and he was fighting a strenuous battle as does a yellowfin. But yellowfins usually travel in schools and the other three rods were as limp as they had been all day.

The thought of a yellowfin did wondrous things for the spectators. We encouraged Perry that he was fighting a splendid ocean creature. It is doubtful that he listened. His mind and body were one in an effort to get whatever he had hooked into the boat.

After a battle of an hour and a half, whatever it was was beginning to give and the spool was again filling with line. Squinting eyes stared deep into the blue water, waiting, hoping to see the long pectoral fins and yellow sides.

But from the ocean's depths came neither the dark blue back, the long pectoral fins, nor yellow sides; instead there came the grey of a black-tipped shark. And one upwards of seventy pounds. The gaff found its mark and the shark was hauled onto the deck, where it thrashed its tail until Joel silenced it with a hammer to the head.

Anyone who has had extensive coastal fishing experience has either hooked or caught a shark. And I will venture to say that many of those sharks caught have probably been left on the beach or destroyed and dropped overboard.

If you have done this—I, too, was once guilty of such—you have missed out on some of the best eating the ocean has to offer: The black tip, sand, dusky and lemon sharks are of excellent quality; the meat is snow white and sweet.

SHARK FROM THE OVEN

2 lbs. shark fillets, cut in serving portions
¾ cup half-and-half cream
1 cup bread crumbs, rolled
¼ cup melted margarine or butter

Salt and pepper fillets to taste; dip in cream, remove and roll in bread crumbs. Brush bottom of baking dish with margarine. Add fish, pour remaining margarine over it and bake 35 to 40 minutes in 350 degree oven, or until fish flakes when tested with fork. Serves 4 to 6.

FRIED SHARK

Fillets for 4
1 egg
2 cups sweet milk
½ t. thyme
2 t. salt
1 t. black pepper
½ cup cracker or corn meal
½ cup vegetable oil

Lightly whip egg; add milk and lightly whip again. Season fish with thyme, salt and pepper. Dip in egg-milk mixture and dust with corn meal. Heat vegetable oil on high heat to bubbling; enter fish, reduce to medium heat and fry 3 to 5 minutes per side. Serves 4.

(Any of the other frying, broiling and baking recipes can be applied to shark cookery.)

COBIA

Cobias do not seem to school in great numbers as do many other saltwater species; yet we have counted up to fifteen in the shade of a buoy.

Most cobias are captured with live eels and are either still-fished on the bottom or near the surface. Some cobia fishermen prefer to search the buoys, where they spot a lounging fish, present a live eel and grunt with appreciation when the fish seizes the long green slimy eel.

Other prefer to troll with standard saltwater spoons; yet others fish with small live blackfish. Crabs are also good bait as are large shrimp.

Tackle should be medium to sturdy. It might also be helpful if the angler is medium to sturdy.

A fairly hefty surf, pier or boat rod spooled with two hundred to two hundred fifty yards of thirty to forty pound test line will help ease the pain when round one begins. The fish can be huge: South Carolina's Broad River near Beaufort yielded a cobia of seventy-eight pounds.

Since cobias are almost toothless, a two-foot leader of eighty-pound monofiliment is sufficient. A sharp 9/0 hook will be suitable for the fight.

Those cobia fishermen who fish the buoys refer to their sport as "cobia hunting." If a cobia is spotted, the bowman makes a short cast in front of the fish and tightens the line—but not too tight—to bring the eel in front of the cobia's jaws.

On occasion a small cobia will dart from beneath the buoy and take the bait quickly. More frequently the fish will take a look-see, nudge the bait and partake of it slowly.

A cobia will release the bait if pressure is applied too soon. Once his mouth clamps shut, set the hook into his jaws. This is easier said than done since the cobia is an expert at spitting out the bait.

When you know the hook has been set, let him have his way. To fight him now is to lose him if he is big. This we wish for no fisherman. If you can, break his head back, turn him opposite to the buoy and back the boat away slowly. Let him run if you are successful in getting him into deep water. It is now a see-saw game: the cobia coming to you, then turning, diving, running. If the hook is properly set the ending will be yours.

Cobias fight like few fish can. Hitting and running deep, then deeper, they maintain a strenuous contest, surrendering only when the last ounce of stamina has been drained.

If you are fishing strictly for the sport, do not gaff the fish, but work him to the boat, reach down with gloved hands and remove the hook from his jaw. If the fish is gut hooked, you have no choice. The fish should be destroyed.

Large cobias grace the trophy rooms of sportfishermen, but small ones, up to ten pounds, indeed, grace a dining table.

FRIED MARINATED COBIA

2 lbs. cobia fillets, cut in serving portions
¼ cup white wine
½ cup vegetable oil
1 cup cracker or corn meal
Salt and pepper

Place fish in bowl, add wine and marinate for 1 hour. Remove, drain, salt, pepper and dust with corn meal. Bring cooking oil to bubbling on high heat; enter fish, reduce to medium and cook 3 to 5 minutes per side. Serve to 4 to 6 with Tartar Sauce. (See Sauces to Accompany Fish.)

BROILED COBIA WITH CREOLE SAUCE

Cobia fillets for 4
¼ cup melted margarine or butter
Salt and pepper

Season fish and baste with margarine. Place on broiler pan and broil 4 inches from coils, 5 to 8 minutes per side. Remove to heated platter and ladle with Creole Sauce. (See Sauces to Accompany Fish for Creole Sauce.) Serves 4.

COBIA ROLL

1 cup cooked, flaked cobia
¼ cup melted margarine, butter or chicken fat
¼ cup all-purpose flour
2 cups chicken stock
1 cup sweet milk
1 2-oz. can mushroom stems and pieces
1 cup canned sweet peas
1 T. pimiento, chopped

In saucepan bring margarine to slow bubble; add flour and blend with wire whip for 2 minutes. Blend in chicken stock, then milk. Remove from stove. Add fish, mushrooms (including liquid), peas and pimiento and fold gently. Pour into bowl and let cool. When cooled, cover bowl and refrigerate at least 3 hours.

Pastry

2 cups all-purpose flour
½ t. salt
¾ cup shortening
5 T. ice water

Prepare pastry 15 minutes before removing cobia mixture from refrigerator. Sift flour into mixing bowl; add salt and shortening. With hands, combine flour and shortening by kneading ingredients together until lumps and beads of dough are removed. Add ice water and continue kneading. Place dough on platter, cover with plastic wrap and refrigerate five minutes. Remove and roll out dough about 18 inches. Ladle fish mixture in center of dough, keeping it at least 2 inches away from perimeter. Roll up pastry. Place on lightly greased cookie or bread pan with smooth side up. Make 3 1-inch slits in center. Brush with melted margarine or butter and place into 400 degree oven. Brush every 15 minutes with margarine until crust browns—35 to 40 minutes. Serves 4 to 6.

FLOUNDER

Flounder, like other fresh and saltwater fish, favor certain locales. Pilings, rocks or reefs that break the current and form eddies are good places to look for them. Rocks along shallow areas of a jetty are excellent feeding areas since the current moves food along the rocks.

The best live bait for flounder is small fish found in the area being fished. Mullets, two to four inches, are good. Live shrimp and mud minnows are also top flounder baits.

When using live mullets or minnows, it is best to hook them through the mouth. Shrimp should be hooked through the head, being careful not to stick the hook through the tiny black spot and kill them.

Flounder have a habit of taking the bait and settling to the bottom. Since the pressure of tidal current against the line can imitate a flounder's tapping, you may be uncertain as to whether it's a picky flounder at line's end or the action of the current. In such an event, wait a few second before setting the hook. If a flounder hits while you are retrieving the line, stop reeling and give the fish slack line before impaling the hook.

Artificials are also highly effective on flounder. Jigs and spoons are among the best when fished near sandbars and oyster beds. Artificials should scrape the bottom since flounder are primarily bottom dwellers.

We don't think we will miss it far if we estimate that ninety percent of the readers who first consult this book will do so in search of how to prepare flounder. As well as its availability through sportfishing, flounder can be found in all seafood and supermarkets.

As is the case with all fish, the fresher the flounder the better. However, it is fortunate that, unlike some fish, flounder do well in the freezer for periods of about six months.

ROLLED FLOUNDER FILLETS

4 flounder fillets from fish 2 to 2½ lbs.
3 T. prepared mustard
1 T. Worcestershire sauce
1 t. thyme
1 t. salt
1 t. black pepper
¾ cup melted margarine or butter

Combine mustard, Worcestershire, thyme, salt and pepper. Spread mixture on each fillet and roll, being careful to keep mixture inside. Secure with toothpicks or twine. Baste with melted margarine and broil 4 inches from coils, 5 to 8 minutes per side, or until meat flakes when tested with fork. Serve to 4.

FLOUNDER VINAIGRETTE

4 fillets from 1½- to 2-lb. flounder
¼ cup melted margarine or butter

Salt and pepper fillets to taste; baste, place on broiler pan 4 inches from coils and broil 5 to 8 minutes per side.

Vinaigrette Dressing

½ cup olive oil
1 T. white vinegar
½ t. celery seed
½ t. salt
1 t. lemon juice
1 clove garlic
Dash thyme

Place ingredients in small saucepan; heat, remove garlic and pour over broiled fillets. Serve to 4.

MARINATED FLOUNDER FILLETS

4 fillets from 2- to 2½-lb. fish
1 cup wine vinegar
Salt, pepper
½ cup cracker or corn meal
½ cup melted margarine or butter

Marinate fillets in wine vinegar for 10 minutes. Remove, salt and pepper to taste and dust with corn meal. Heat margarine on high heat to bubbling; enter fish, reduce heat to medium and cook 5 to 8 minutes per side. Serves 4.

FLOUNDER STUFFED WITH SHRIMP

1 2½- to 3-lb. flounder
¼ cup melted margarine or butter
Salt and pepper

Begin at base of gill of flounder and cut down backbone to thick part of tail. Fillet, both sides, back about 1 inch. Fill with stuffing. (See Shrimp Stuffing under Breads and Stuffings.) Baste with margarine, salt and pepper and broil 5 minutes per pound per side. Serve to 4.

(A white wine or cheese sauce also enhances the flavor of flounder. See Sauces to Accompany Fish.)

Part III

Shellfish

SHRIMP

Shrimping is best on a rising tide. If the bottom permits, and the area is accessible by foot, some shrimpers wade for their catch. Equipment for them is a net cast by hand, a net which takes quite a bit of practice. Shrimping from a boat is safer than shrimping by wading since sharks do inhabit the same waters.

Unlike clams or crabs or oysters, shrimp are easier to clean. There is, however, a black vein (intestine) that runs down the shrimp's back. Some people leave this vein as it is and others remove it. This is strictly a matter of choice for it harms neither the flavor nor you if the vein is not removed.

For added flavor leave heads intact when boiling. After the shrimp have boiled, remove heads, shuck free of shell and eat. For frying fresh (green) shrimp, remove heads, discard shells and fry. Be certain that shrimp are free of strong odor before boiling or frying.

BOILED SHRIMP

2 lbs. green shrimp
3 cups water
1 T. salt
½ T. black pepper
1 whole lemon, halved

Place water, salt, pepper and lemon into pot; cover and bring to boil for 5 minutes. Add shrimp, return to second boil, reduce heat to medium and cook 15 minutes. Drain, shell and serve with your favorite cocktail sauce. (See Sauces to Accompany Fish.) Serves 4 to 6.

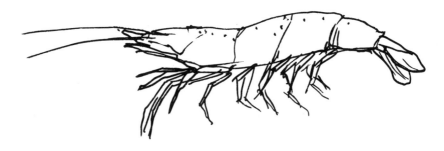

SHRIMP CREOLE

1 lb. boiled shrimp
1 bell pepper, diced
1 medium onion, diced
1 rib of celery, diced
1 No. 303 can tomatoes
1 cup water
1 small can tomato sauce
1 T. Worcestershire sauce
Dash Tabasco sauce
2 chicken bouillon cubes
Salt and pepper to taste

In 1 cup water, cook bell pepper, onion and celery until tender. Add tomatoes, tomato sauce, Worcestershire and Tabasco. Let ingredients simmer 30 minutes. Add shrimp, salt, pepper and undiluted bouillon cubes. Let simmer for 15 minutes. Served over steamed rice to 4.

ANOTHER SHRIMP CREOLE

1 lb. boiled shrimp, halved
1 bell pepper, sliced
1 medium onion, sliced
1 clove garlic, finely chopped
2 T. margarine or butter, melted
1 10½-oz. can condensed tomato soup
⅓ cup water
2 t. lemon juice
¼ t. salt
Dash black pepper
Dash Tabasco sauce

In melted margarine, cook bell pepper, onion and garlic in skillet over medium heat until tender. Add remaining ingredients and simmer for 12 minutes. Serve over steamed rice. Serves 4 to 6.

FRIED SHRIMP

2 lbs. fresh shrimp, cleaned
1 cup vegetable oil
1 egg
1 cup sweet milk
2 cups cracker meal

In soup bowl, beat egg lightly and combine with milk. Dip shrimp into mixture and dust with cracker meal. Bring vegetable oil to bubbling on high heat; add shrimp, reduce to medium and cook 3 to 5 minutes. Serves 4 to 6.

SHRIMP AND RICE

1 lb. boiled shrimp
1 cup long grain and wild rice mixture
2½ cups water
1 t. salt
1 2½-oz. can sliced or button mushrooms
1 cup canned garden peas

Place water in pot, add salt, bring to boil. Add rice, stir and reduce to low heat. Cover and cook 30 minutes. **Do not open pot during this time.** When rice is done, fluff it up and stir in shrimp, mushrooms and peas. Cover and let stand 5 minutes. Serves 4.

LOW-COUNTRY SHRIMP BOIL

1 lb. shrimp for boiling
6 ears uncooked corn
6 smoked sausages
2 lemons, halved
1 T. salt
1 t. black pepper
1 qt. water

Bring water seasoned with salt, pepper and lemons to boil in large pot. Add sausages, cover, reduce heat to medium and cook 10 minutes. Add shrimp and corn and cook 10 minutes. Drain and serve to 4.

(You could also include clams and crabs in this popular South Carolina dish.)

SHRIMP NEWBURG

1 lb. boiled shrimp added to 1½ cups Newburg Sauce. [See Sauces to Accompany Fish.]

Serve on toast points to 4.

BELL PEPPERS STUFFED WITH SHRIMP

1 lb. boiled shrimp, sliced in half
4 medium bell peppers, tops removed and seeded
½ cup cooked rice
¼ cup ketchup
1 t. Worcestershire sauce
1 No. 303 can tomatoes
½ cup onion sauteed in 1 T. vegetable oil

Blanch peppers. In mixing bowl, combine shrimp, rice, ketchup, Worcestershire sauce and onion. Mix well. Stuff peppers and place in casserole dish. Top each pepper with a tomato. Pour juice from tomatoes into bottom of dish. Place in preheated 350 degree oven 45 minutes. Spoon pan juice over peppers every 15 minutes. Serves 4.

SHRIMP ROLL

See Cobia Roll (Saltwater Fish) and complete recipe as directed, substituting shrimp for fish.

SHRIMP BISQUE

1½ lbs. boiled shrimp, chopped
4 cups sweet milk
½ cup celery, diced
⅓ cup all-purpose flour
⅓ cup margarine or butter
1 T. sherry

Pour milk and celery into saucepan. Heat slowly so as not to burn. In another saucepan, melt margarine or butter on medium heat. Add flour and blend with margarine. Add milk, celery mixture into flour base and blend with wire ship on medium heat. Add shrimp, salt and pepper to taste. Bring to slow boil, stirring. Add sherry, stir and serve to 4 in heated soup bowls.

JAMBALAYA

1 lb. boiled shrimp, chopped
¼ cup chopped breakfast bacon, uncooked
3 T. onion, chopped
3 T. bell pepper, chopped
1 clove garlic, finely chopped
1 T. all-purpose flour
1 t. salt
Dash cayenne
Dash paprika
½ t. Worcestershire sauce
2 cups canned tomatoes
2 cups cooked rice

Fry bacon in skillet until crisp. Add onion, bell pepper and garlic and cook until tender. Blend in flour. Add seasonings, tomatoes and cook on medium heat, stirring until thick. Stir in rice and shrimp. Heat and serve to 6.

SKILLET SHRIMP

1 lb. fresh cleaned shrimp
¼ cup vegetable oil or shortening
1 small bell pepper, chopped
1 2-oz. can mushroom stems and pieces
½ t. salt
¼ t. black pepper

Bring vegetable oil or shortening to high heat in skillet. Add mushrooms and bell pepper; reduce to medium heat and sauté 3 minutes.
Add shrimp, salt, pepper and sauté 3 to 5 minutes. Serve on lightly
buttered noodles to 4.

SEAFOOD ROLL

¼ cup boiled shrimp
¼ cup crab meat
¼ cup minced clams
¼ cup chopped oysters

See Cobia Roll (Saltwater Fish) and complete recipe as directed.

SHRIMP GUMBO

1 lb. fresh cleaned shrimp
2 cups okra, sliced
⅓ cup vegetable oil
⅔ cup green onions, chopped [including tops]
1 clove garlic, finely chopped
1½ t. salt
½ t. black pepper
2 cups hot water
1 cup canned tomatoes
2 whole bay leaves
½ t. Tabasco sauce
1 cup cooked rice

In 1-quart cooking pot, cook okra in vegetable oil on medium heat,
stirring, for 3 minutes. Add onion, garlic, salt, pepper and shrimp.
Cook, stirring, 5 minutes. Add water, tomatoes, bay leaves and
Tabasco. Cover and simmer 20 minutes. Remove bay leaves. Place
¼ cup cooked rice in each of soup bowls; fill with gumbo. Serves 4.

CURRIED SHRIMP

1 lb. fresh shelled shrimp
2 cups water
1 t. salt
½ t. black pepper
1 whole bay leaf
1 T. onion, finely chopped
1½ T. margarine or butter
1½ T. all-purpose flour
½ cup onion, chopped
1 garlic clove, finely chopped
1 t. salt
1½ T. curry powder
1 cup canned whole tomatoes, chopped
1 T. lemon juice

Place shrimp in pot; add water, salt, pepper, bay leaf and onion. Bring to boil, cover, reduce to medium heat and cook 4 minutes. Strain and reserve 1½ cups shrimp broth.

In skillet—medium heat—melt margarine or butter; add onions and cook until tender. While stirring, add garlic, salt, flour and curry powder. Cook 3 minutes, stirring. Add tomatoes, lemon juice and shrimp broth. Stir. Reduce heat to simmer and cook 10 to 12 minutes, covered. Add shrimp, heat and serve to 4 over steamed rice.

CREAMED SHRIMP

1 lb. boiled shrimp
2 cups medium white sauce [See Sauces to Accompany Fish.]
½ t. celery salt
1 T. pimiento, chopped

Add boiled shrimp to white sauce; fold in celery salt and pimiento. Heat and serve on toast points or in pastry shells. Serves 4 to 6. (Mushrooms may be added, if desired.)

CRABS

Blue crabs comprise the vast majority of the catch by recreational crabbers. You can find blue crabs deep in the marsh creeks around piers, bridge pilings and entrances to most saltwater bayous where there is a flow of water.

While some prefer to use a line baited with a piece of fish (mullet heads are best) the easiest method is to use a wire trap, available at most sporting and hardware stores in coastal regions. The baited trap is lowered to the bottom and the sides automatically drop down, allowing the crabs to swim in to eat. At about fifteen-minute intervals, snatch hard on the line fastened to the trap to close the doors and trap the crabs.

The most important thing to remember about crabs is to cook immediately after catching them, especially during hot weather. **Do not cook dead crabs**. The internal parts of a crab are associated with the meat itself, resulting in a quick breakdown of chemicals within the body when the crab dies. An upset stomach could result from eating dead crabs.

Cooked crabs placed on ice will keep two days.

Crabbing is not a chore but cleaning them is. Since blue crabs are hard shelled, they must be boiled before the meat can be removed. This is done by placing them in hot water seasoned with salt and lemons or limes and boiling. Although you can purchase special seasonings for cooking crabs, plain salt is just as satisfactory. Fresh lemons or limes can be used or you can substitute the bottled concentrates.

When the water comes to a bubbling boil, drop live crabs into the pot; let the water return to a boil, then reduce heat to medium. Allow twenty to thirty minutes for cooking.

To remove the meat, break off the claws and legs and crack with a nutcracker. To remove body meat (lump), lay crab on top shell, insert index finger or, if necessary, the point of a knife, under the end of the flap that folds under the body from the rear. Break off and discard. With both hands, pull upper and lower shell apart. Discard top shell, and the spongy white fibers. The rest is edible. Clean with freshwater and pick out meat with a fork. A nutpick is excellent for removing meat that is difficult to reach. You can eat the meat as is or prepare one of the following recipes. The white lump meat removed from the body is the most desirable. Claw meat is light colored and is excellent. Use lump meat for deviled crabs, casseroles and soups, and claw meat for salads.

It is now illegal to take "she" (female) crabs in South Carolina, so one must be content with the "he" (male) crabs.

How does one tell the she from the he? On the apron (belly) of the male crab, the tail is long, pointed and fits into a groove. The female crab's tail is wide and rounded on the forward end. Remember, too, that crabs smaller than five inches, measured from the top of the point across the back of the shell, are unlawful to take while crabbing in South Carolina. Check with state wildlife departments before crabbing.

DEVILED CRABS

1 lb. crab meat
1 small onion, chopped
2 T. bell pepper, chopped
½ cup celery, chopped
1 fresh lemon or 1 T. lemon concentrate
Dash Tabasco sauce
Dash Worcestershire sauce
1 egg
1 t. prepared mustard
2 T. vegetable oil
1 cup vegetable oil
20 saltine crackers, crushed fine

In small saucepan, cook onion, celery and bell pepper in 2 tablespoons oil on medium heat until tender. Do not brown. When done, empty into mixing bowl. Add lemon juice, Worcestershire and Tabasco sauce. Fold. Add crab meat, egg and mustard. Add small amount of cracker crumbs at a time until mixture is workable. Heat oil on high heat until it bubbles in skillet or electric fry pan. Shape mixture into individual patties, place in pan, reduce heat to medium and cook 3 to 5 minutes per side. Serves 4 to 6.

CAROLINA "SHE-CRAB" SOUP

1 cup crab meat
1 pt. sweet milk
1 pt. half-and-half
¼ stick of margarine or butter
1 T. sherry
Peel of ½ lemon
Yolks from 2 hard-boiled eggs [Since it is now illegal to use
    female crabs, we must improvise with egg yolks to replace
    crab eggs.]
10 saltine crackers, rolled fine

Pour milk in top of double boiler with lemon peel and let simmer 5
minutes. Add crab, margarine, cream, salt and pepper to taste and
crumbled egg yolks. Simmer 15 to 20 minutes. Thicken with cracker
crumbs. Heat sherry separately and pour equal portions in each of 4
to 6 bowls. Pour crab soup over the sherry. Serves 4 to 6.

CRAB NEWBURG

1 cup crab meat

See Sauces to Accompany Fish for Newburg Sauce. Serve to 4 on
toast or in pastry shells.

CRAB CASSEROLE

1 cup crab meat
1 can condensed mushroom soup
1 can sweet milk
¼ cup mild cheese, grated
¼ cup rolled saltine crackers [10 crackers]

Empty soup into saucepan; add milk, stir, and bring to bubbling on
medium heat. Add cheese and stir until melted. Fold in crab meat.
Heat thoroughly. Pour into casserole dish. Top with cracker crumbs
and bake in 400 degree oven until browned. Serves 4.

SAUTÉED CRAB

1 cup crab meat
1 medium bell pepper, halved and cut into strips
1 2½-oz. can button mushrooms
1 clove garlic
2 T. margarine or butter

In skillet melt margarine or butter on medium heat. Add whole peeled garlic clove and bell pepper. Sauté 3 minutes; remove garlic and discard. Add mushrooms (reserve liquid) and sauté for 3 minutes. Add crab meat and mushroom juice and sauté until meat is heated. Remove and serve over steamed rice to 4.

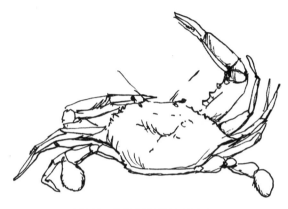

CRAB OMELET FOR TWO

¼ cup flaked crab meat
1 T. bell pepper, chopped
1 T. onion, chopped
1 T. vegetable oil
4 eggs
4 t. margarine or butter

Sauté pepper and onion in vegetable oil until tender. Remove and drain excess oil from pepper and onion. Beat 2 eggs lightly in small bowl; pour into medium-heated pan with 2 teaspoons melted margarine or butter. When eggs begin to cook, begin moving pan from side to side in a rapid motion to keep them from sticking. Line center of omelet with half of the measured crab meat and half of the sautéed pepper and onion. Fold over. Brown on both sides and place on heated platter. Repeat for second omelet. (If you like, you may serve either with a Wine, Cheese or Newburg Sauce.) Garnish omelets with freshly sliced tomatoes.

MATT'S CRAB-SHRIMP THERMIDOR

This recipe calls for fresh crabs since the mixture is placed into the crab shells for serving. If time does not allow you to go crabbing, most seafood markets, on order, can obtain the shells for you.

1 lb. crab meat
1 lb. boiled shrimp, chopped
1 medium bell pepper, chopped fine
¼ cup celery, chopped fine
¼ cup onion, chopped fine
2 T. margarine or butter
1 T. parsley flakes
1 t. prepared mustard
1 t. Worcestershire sauce
½ cup sherry
1 cup buttered bread crumbs
1½ cups cream sauce

Cream Sauce

2 T. margarine or butter
2 T. all-purpose flour
1 cup sweet milk or half-and-half
¼ t. salt
1/8 t. black pepper

Melt margarine or butter in saucepan over medium heat. Add flour, stir and cook until blended—about 2 minutes. Heat milk and add to flour mixture. Cook, stirring, until thickened. Add salt and pepper; stir. Remove and place in double boiler to keep warm

Sauté bell pepper, onion and celery in butter or margarine until tender. Remove, pour into bowl and add parsley, mustard, Worcestershire, sherry and cream sauce. Mix together. Add crab and shrimp meat. Mix well. Fill 6 to 8 crab shells. Cover with buttered bread crumbs and brown in 350 degree oven. Garnish with lemon or lime wedges. Serves 6 to 8.

OYSTERS

We do not know in what order oysters appeared in the scheme of things, but prehistoric coastal Indians found them favorable as can be attested to by the massive shell rings found around their dwellings. Some of these shell rings are reported to be more than a hundred feet in diameter and contain tens of thousands of bushels of sun-bleached shells, dating as early as about 2000 B.C.

We've often wondered about the foods we now eat as to what individual might first have sampled to see what was fit or not fit to eat. It must have been a brave soul who first sampled oysters on the half shell. And to that individual we owe a debt of thanks.

Those of you who have never mucked about a saltwater flat at low tide and consumed raw oysters have not been treated to the true, unblemished oyster flavor. Store-bought oysters, and we've purchased our share, lose considerable flavor during the washing process.

If you're for the first time encountering an oyster tightly sealed in its shelled home, follow this simple procedure to make it open its door.

While you can use a pocket or hunting knife—or even a table knife—an oyster knife is by far the best utensil to use. Gloves? Definitely. A pair of cotton work gloves will suffice.

Place the oyster—flat side down—on a nonslippery surface and hold it firmly with your hand. With the thin end facing you, press the point of the oyster knife down, then insert and slide from left to right as you pry. This will sever the muscle and force the oyster to give.

The oyster, when opened, should be creamy in color and void of odor. The oyster should also secrete a fluid when the knife enters the shell. If any one of these factors is missing, discard the oyster. **Do not eat.**

We have read that oystermen can distinguish the sex of oysters and recommend that the females be fried and the males stewed. We consider ourselves to be an equal-opportunity cook, and as such, have no preference.

Oysters, especially those gathered by hand or purchased fresh from the docks, should need no salting as they are naturally seasoned. Oysters that have already been shelled have been washed and need salting before cooking.

FRIED OYSTERS

4 dozen shucked and ready-to-cook oysters
2 cups cracker or corn meal
2 cups vegetable oil

In skillet or electric fry pan bring oil to bubbling. Do not reduce heat. Dust oysters lightly with meal and place in oil. Fry until oysters are golden, no more than 3 minutes. Serves 4.

(Variations of this fried oyster: marinate oysters in either ½ cup lemon or lime juice 5 minutes prior to mealing.)

BOYKIN'S FRIED OYSTERS

4 dozen ready-to-cook oysters
2 cups cracker or corn meal
2 cups vegetable oil
2 eggs
1 T. water

Break eggs into bowl, add water and whip lightly. Dust oysters with meal, dip into egg mixture and dust again. Place on cookie sheet, cover with plastic wrap and refrigerate 1 hour. Remove and fry as above. Serves 4.

OYSTER STEW FOR TWO

2 cups sweet milk
½ pt. oysters, drained
½ T. margarine or butter
1 t. salt
½ t. black pepper

In saucepan add milk, oysters, salt and pepper. Bring to slow boil, stirring to keep milk from scorching. Add margarine or butter and continue to stir until melted. Remove from stove and pour into heated bowls. You may wish to garnish with paprika. (Some persons prefer to make a red stew by adding a teaspoon of ketchup in each bowl of stew.)

RICH OYSTER STEW FOR TWO

½ pt. oysters, drained
2 cups half-and-half
½ T. margarine or butter
1 t. salt
½ t. black pepper
Dash of nutmeg

Follow above directions for preparation.

OYSTER BISQUE

1 pt. oysters with liquor
1 pt. sweet milk
1 pt. cream
¼ stick of margarine or butter
1 t. sherry
2 t. salt
½ t. black pepper
Peel of ½ lemon
1 cup rolled saltine cracker crumbs

Drain oysters, reserving liquor, and chop fine. In deep saucepan add milk, cream and lemon peel. Bring to slow boil. Let boil for 1 minute while stirring; remove and discard lemon peel. Continue stirring and add oysters, liquor and margarine or butter. Stir in salt and pepper. Let cook on low heat, stirring, for 3 minutes. Remove and thicken with cracker crumbs. Add sherry and serve to 4.

ANOTHER OYSTER BISQUE

1 pt. oysters with liquor
2 cups water
1 small onion, chopped fine
¼ cup celery, diced
1 t. parsley flakes
1 bay leaf

Chop oysters and place in saucepan with liquor; add water, onion, parsley, celery and bay leaf. Bring to medium boil, then reduce heat to simmer and cook for 20 to 25 minutes.

Cream Sauce

2 cups sweet milk
1 T. margarine or butter
1 T. all-purpose flour
½ t. salt
1/8 t. black pepper
1 cup saltine cracker crumbs

Place milk in double boiler and heat. Add cracker crumbs and cook for 20 minutes. Melt margarine or butter in saucepan and blend in flour, salt and pepper. Cook until ingredients begin to thicken on medium heat. Add milk-crumb mixture gradually, stirring constantly. Cook 2 to 3 minutes. Gradually stir white sauce mixture into oysters until blended. More milk or cream may be added if bisque is thicker than desired. Float thin slices of lemon on top of bisque when served to 6. (A dash of paprika also enhances this dish.)

CORN-OYSTER FRITTERS

¼ cup oysters, chopped
2 eggs
1 t. salt
½ t. black pepper
1 T. onion, finely chopped
3 T. all-purpose flour
1 cup canned corn
1 cup vegetable oil

In bowl, beat eggs until thick; add onions, salt and pepper, corn and oysters. Mix well. Add flour in small amounts, mixing, until mixture is smooth. Bring vegetable oil to bubbling on high heat. Drop spoonfuls into hot oil, reduce to medium heat and cook 3 to 5 minutes. Serves 4 to 6.

OVEN-STEAMED OYSTERS

1 dozen oysters in shell, scrubbed
1 cup water

Place oysters in baking pan, add water and place into 400 degree oven. Oysters should pop open in about 5 minutes. Eat them as they are or serve with a cocktail sauce. (See Sauces to Accompany Fish.)

BROILED OYSTERS

1 dozen oysters, scrubbed and open to the half shell
2 T. margarine or butter, melted
Salt and pepper to taste
Garlic salt

Salt and pepper each oyster, sprinkle lightly with garlic salt and dot each oyster with melted margarine or butter. Place oysters on cookie sheet and under broiler 4 inches from coils for 3 minutes. Remove and serve with lemon or lime wedges.

OYSTER CHOWDER

½ pt. oysters in liquor
2 cups sweet milk
1 t. salt
½ t. black pepper
½ medium onion, chopped
1 rib celery, chopped thin
1½ T. margarine or butter
2 cups water
1 medium potato, diced

Melt margarine in deep pot, add onion and sauté until tender. Add water, celery, potatoes, salt and pepper. Cover, bring to boil, reduce heat to medium and cook until celery is tender but not mushy. Add oysters, liquor and milk. Cook 5 minutes and serve to 4.

SCALLOPED OYSTERS

1 pt. oysters
¾ cup dry bread crumbs
¾ cup cracker crumbs
½ t. salt
Dash black pepper
½ cup margarine or butter, melted
¼ t. Worcestershire sauce
1 cup sweet milk

Drain oysters. Combine crumbs—bread and cracker—salt, pepper and margarine or butter. Sprinkle ⅓ of buttered, seasoned crumbs into casserole dish. Cover with a layer of oysters. Repeat layers. Add Worcestershire sauce to milk; pour over oysters. Sprinkle remaining crumbs over top. Bake in 400 degree oven 20 to 25 minutes or until brown. Serves 4 to 6.

OYSTERS CASINO

1 pt. oysters
3 slices uncooked breakfast bacon, chopped
4 T. onion, chopped
2 T. bell pepper, chopped
2 T. celery, chopped
1 t. lemon juice
½ t. salt
1/8 t. black pepper
½ t. Worcestershire sauce
2 drops Tabasco sauce

Fry bacon on medium heat; add onion, bell pepper and celery and cook until tender. Add remaining seasonings and mix. Place oysters in buttered baking dish. Spread bacon mixture over oysters. Bake at 350 degrees 10 minutes or until brown. Serves 4 to 6.

OYSTERS FROM THE PAN

1 pt. oysters in liquor
4 T. margarine or butter
1 t. salt
½ t. black pepper
1 t. Worcestershire sauce
Dash Tabasco sauce

Place oysters and liquor in pan at medium heat. Add salt and pepper and cook until edges of oysters begin to curl. Add margarine or butter, Worcestershire and Tabasco sauce. Fold until margarine has melted and mixture returns to bubbling. Remove and serve over lightly buttered toast to 4. Ring with lemon wedges.

OYSTERS A LA KING

1 pt. oysters
¼ cup celery, diced
¼ cup bell pepper, diced
4 T. margarine or butter
4 T. all-purpose flour
2 cups sweet milk
1 egg, beaten
1 T. pimiento, chopped
1 t. salt
1/8 t. black pepper

In saucepan, simmer oysters in their liquor for about 5 minutes or until edges begin to curl. Drain. In another pan, cook celery and bell pepper in margarine on medium heat until tender. Blend in flour, add milk and cook on medium heat until thick, stirring constantly. Into beaten egg, stir in a little of the hot sauce (1 tablespoon). Then add egg mixture to sauce, stirring. Add oysters and remaining seasonings and heat, stirring throughly. Serve over pastry shells or toast points to 6.

CLAMS

Clams are divided into two categories: soft- and hard-shell. The soft-shell clam is found north of Cape Cod and is usually steamed or eaten raw on the half shell. These clams are easily opened by sliding a sharp knife across the top shell. (You should open them over a bowl in order to retain the juices, which can later be used to prepare clam chowder.) The meat of the clam is encased in a tough hide. Make a small incision from the top of the meat to the bottom. Grasp the clam meat in one hand and pull the skin free with the other. The skin, though too tough to eat, can be ground for use in clam chowder.

Hard-shell clams include butter clams and quahogs. The junior-sized clams are also referred to as cherrystones and medium-sized clams are called littlenecks. The larger quahogs are strongly flavored and used for chowders. The smaller clams are served on the half shell.

Quahogs are quite stubborn to open. Covering them with cold water for several minutes will relax them so that you can insert a knife in the opening. The heat of a moderate oven will also force them to open, but this may result in a loss of flavor.

Remember that all clams are sandy and should be scrubbed in several waters. A hard-bristle toothbrush is an excellent utensil for this purpose.

When the clam is opened, remove the black interior of the shellfish. The remaining meat is edible.

Hard-shell clams are best when used for chowder and soft-shell clams are usually better for steaming or frying. A rule of thumb for estimating quantities of clams in the shell: 8 quarts of unshucked clams yield 1 quart of dressed clams.

FRIED CLAMS

1 qt. shucked clams [reserve liquor]
1 egg, beaten
1 t. salt
½ t. black pepper
2 cups cracker or corn meal
2 cups vegetable oil or shortening

Drain clams and reserve 2 tablespoons liquor. Combine liquor with egg, salt and pepper. Dip clams in egg mixture, dust with cracker meal and fry in hot oil 4 to 5 minutes. Drain on paper towels. Serves 4 to 6.

NEW ENGLAND CLAM CHOWDER

2 cups clams, chopped
2 cups clam liquor
2 slices uncooked breakfast bacon, chopped
2 T. margarine or butter
2 cups sweet milk
1 large onion, chopped
2 cups raw potatoes, diced
Salt and pepper to taste

Place bacon in kettle or soup pot; heat to medium and cook 10 minutes. Add onions and cook until tender. Add clams, potatoes, salt and pepper. Cover with water and cook until potatoes are easily pierced when tested with fork. Add clam liquor and milk and cook 10 minutes. Serves 4 to 6.

MANHATTAN CLAM CHOWDER

1 cup clams, chopped
1 cup clam juice
2 slices uncooked breakfast bacon, chopped
1 medium bell pepper, chopped
1 medium onion, chopped
1 16-oz. can tomatoes or 2 cups ketchup
3 cups water
1 carrot, chopped
2 celery ribs, chopped
2 t. salt
1 t. black pepper

In kettle or soup pot, cook bacon on medium heat for 10 minutes. Add onions and bell pepper and cook until tender. Add water, celery and tomatoes. Cook 15 minutes on medium heat, covered. Add salt, pepper, carrots, clams and clam liquor. Cook 20 minutes on medium heat, covered. Serves 4.

CLAM CASSEROLE WITH SHERRY

2 dozen clams, shucked
1 cup sweet milk or cream
½ cup sherry
½ cup cracker crumbs
½ T. melted margarine or butter
Salt, pepper

Grease casserole dish with melted margarine or butter. Salt and pepper clams to taste and layer. Sprinkle lightly with cracker crumbs. Add ½ milk or cream and ½ sherry. Repeat until clams are used. Bake in 350 degree oven 35 to 40 minutes. Serves 4.

DEVILED CLAMS ON THE HALF SHELL

1 cup clams, minced [reserve shells]
1 small onion, chopped fine
2 T. bell pepper, finely chopped
½ cup celery, finely chopped
1 fresh lemon or 1 T. concentrated lemon juice
Dash of Tabasco sauce
Dash of Worcestershire sauce
2 T. vegetable oil
1 egg
2 t. prepared mustard
10 saltine crackers, crushed fine

Cook onion, celery and bell pepper in vegetable oil on medium heat 5 minutes, stirring. Do not brown. When cooked, add lemon juice, Worcestershire and Tabasco sauce. Stir and pour into mixing bowl. Add minced clams and rolled cracker crumbs and fold gently with mustard. Spoon mixture into shells and bake at 350 degrees 25 to 30 minutes. Serves 4 to 6. (A topping of grated Parmesan cheese enhances the flavor.)

CLAM FRITTERS

1 cup clams, minced
½ cup sweet milk
½ cup half-and-half
1 T. melted margarine or butter
2 cups all-purpose flour
1 T. baking powder
1 t. salt
1 cup vegetable oil or shortening

Sift flour, salt and baking powder into mixing bowl. In soup bowl, beat eggs lightly, add to flour and mix. Add milk and half-and-half and stir until smooth. Blend in melted margarine or butter. Fold in minced clams. Heat vegetable oil on high heat to bubbling. Drop mixture (teaspoon portions) into hot oil. Reduce to medium and fry 3 to 5 minutes or until fritters have browned. Serves 4 to 6.

BAKED CLAM HASH

1 pt. clams, chopped
⅓ cup uncooked breakfast bacon, chopped
½ cup onion, chopped
2 cups cooked potatoes, diced
¼ cup parsley, chopped
2 eggs, beaten
2 t. salt
1 t. black pepper
1 t. paprika

In skillet, fry bacon on medium heat until crisp. Remove bacon and drain on paper towels. Cook onion in fat until tender. Add clams and cook 5 minutes. Pour onions and clams into bowl; add remaining ingredients, except bacon and paprika. Place clam mixture into casserole dish. Top with paprika and bacon. Bake at 350 degrees 30 to 35 minutes. Serves 4 to 6.

Part IV

Sauces to Accompany Fish

We do not know when sauces gained popular acceptance, but we have read that they were used to mask the flavor of non-too-fresh foods in the days before refrigeration. Today, sauces are used to our advantage to enhance both the flavor and appearance of foods.

The French have long experimented with sauces and are considered masters of the art. The Chinese are credited with the popular sweet-and-sour sauces and India has given us the curries. Whatever the origination, we are also grateful to those epicures who gave us the Newburg, Hollandaise, butter and cocktail sauces which accompany our seafood dishes.

We know of no other sauces more pleasing to the eye and more adaptable to fish cookery than the basic white sauce.

BASIC WHITE SAUCE

¼ cup margarine or butter
¼ cup all-purpose flour
1 t. salt
2 cups sweet milk
1 T. sherry [optional]

In heavy-bottom saucepan, melt margarine over low heat. Blend in flour vigorously with a wire whip and cook slowly.

(The secret to achieving a smooth white sauce is to remove the pan of melted margarine or butter from the heat before blending in the flour. When the flour is blended over heat it tends to lump.) Continue stirring to prevent further lumping and to keep flour from burning. At the precise second the paste turns a very light, almond color, remove, gradually stirring, and add milk. Return to stove and add salt.

If wine is added, do not let sauce come to a boil. This impairs the delicate wine flavor.

If the sauce is reheated, use a double boiler to prevent it from sticking and scorching.

White sauce accentuates the flavor of broiled or baked fish. You might try adding a teaspoon of chicken stock to the sauce. Also, a teaspoon of nutmeg lends a robust accent. Finely chopped parsley, the green stalks from fresh spring onions and chopped or stripped pimiento provide eye-appeal.

ORANGE SAUCE

Although this sauce usually accompanies meats, both wild and domesticated, it is also suitable for baked or poached fish. With the recent impact of Chinese cookery in this country, sweet sauces are increasingly seen on our tables.

1 cup orange juice
¼ cup sugar [sugar substitutes will suffice]
1 t. nutmeg
Cornstarch to thicken [approx. 1 T.]
1 T. sherry [optional]

In medium saucepan combine orange juice, sugar and nutmeg. Bring to a rolling boil, add cornstarch and stir. Remove from heat, add sherry if desired, and spoon over baked, broiled or poached fish.

MUSHROOM SAUCE

¼ **cup margarine or butter**
¼ **cup all-purpose flour**
1 t. salt
¼ **t. black pepper**
2 cups sweet milk
1 chicken bouillon cube
1 2-oz. can mushroom stems and pieces, with liquid
1 t. Worcestershire sauce
1 T. pimiento, chopped

Make basic White Sauce and fold in additional ingredients. Tasty when served either with broiled, baked or poached fish.

NEWBURG SAUCE

3 T. margarine or butter
1 T. all-purpose flour
Dash nutmeg
Dash paprika
¼ **t. salt**
1 cup light cream
½ **cup sweet milk**
2 egg yolks
1 T. sherry
1 2-oz. can mushroom stems and pieces [optional]

Melt margarine or butter in saucepan. Remove from heat and stir in flour, nutmeg, paprika and salt. Return to heat and stir until paste is smooth. Pour in cream and milk and stir. In small soup bowl, beat egg yolks lightly with sherry. Fold into sauce, add mushrooms and heat thoroughly while continuing to stir. Serve over broiled, baked or poached fish.

(If making a shrimp newburg, add cooked boiled shrimp last. Leave on heat only long enough for shrimp to heat thoroughly.)

CHEESE SAUCE

2 T. margarine or butter
1½ T. all-purpose flour
1 cup sweet milk
¼ cup mild cheddar cheese, grated

Melt margarine or butter in saucepan over medium heat. Add flour and blend with wire whip 2 minutes. While stirring, pour in milk. Add cheese and continue stirring until cheese has melted. Zesty with baked, broiled and poached fish.

LEMON-CHIVE SAUCE

⅔ cup margarine or butter
3 T. chives, chopped
2 T. lemon juice
2 t. lemon peel, grated
½ t. salt
⅓ t. black pepper

Melt margarine or butter in saucepan. Add remaining ingredients. Mix thoroughly and pour over baked, broiled or poached fish. Sensational!

HOLLANDAISE

This sauce is supreme with poached fish.

2 egg yolks
¼ cup margarine or butter, melted
¼ cup boiling water
1 T. lemon juice
¼ t. salt
Dash of Cayenne

Water in bottom pan of double boiler should be no more than 1 inch deep. You do not want water to touch upper pot.

Bring water to boil on high heat; reduce to medium heat. In top pan of double boiler, beat eggs lightly with wire whip. Stir in melted margarine or butter. Add boiling water slowly, stirring constantly until sauce thickens. Remove immediately; stir in lemon juice, salt and cayenne.

OYSTER SAUCE

1 cup oysters with liquor
¼ cup margarine or butter
¼ cup all-purpose flour
1 t. salt
1 cup cream or half-and-half

Cook oysters with liquor in 1 tablespoon margarine or butter until oysters curl. Remove oysters and chop. Add cream or half-and-half to oyster liquor to make 2 cups sauce. In saucepan, add remaining margarine or butter and melt. Remove pan, gradually add flour, blend with wire whip and return to heat until paste has formed. Add oyster sauce and stir. Remove from heat, add salt and chopped oysters. A treat for poached, baked or broiled fish.

CREOLE SAUCE

1 bell pepper, diced
1 medium onion, diced
1 celery rib, diced
1 cup tomatoes, chopped
1 small can tomato sauce
1 T. Worcestershire sauce
2 chicken bouillon cubes

Cook bell pepper, onion and celery in 1 cup water until tender. Add tomatoes, tomato sauce and Worcestershire. Let ingredients simmer for 30 minutes and add bouillon cubes. Salt and pepper to taste. Let simmer for 15 minutes. Recommended for broiled fish.

TARTAR SAUCE

½ cup bell pepper, finely chopped
½ cup dill pickle, finely chopped
1 medium onion, finely chopped
½ cup mayonnaise
½ t. paprika
Juice from 1 lemon

Place bell pepper, dill pickle and onion on a dish towel and squeeze out all liquid. Place in mixing bowl and add lemon juice, paprika and mayonnaise. (Mayonnaise should be added in small amounts to assure that consistency doesn't become too thin.) Excellent with fried, broiled, baked or poached fish; fried oysters; shrimp; clams.

GARLIC SAUCE

Garlic, a bulbous-rooted plant of the onion family, has a distinct aroma and accentuates the flavor of many foods.

2 T. margarine or butter
1 clove garlic, minced
½ t. parsley flakes [optional]

Melt margarine or butter in saucepan. Add garlic and let simmer 3 minutes. Strain and serve over poached, baked or broiled fish. Parsley flakes may be added for color. This sauce can also be used as a cocktail sauce dip for boiled shrimp or steamed oysters on the half shell.

COCKTAIL SAUCES AND DIPS

A cocktail sauce is sometimes indistinguishable from a dip. Both are served with boiled shrimp, crabs and raw or steamed oysters and clams. Cocktail sauces need not be complicated to do honor to both the foods being served and to the hostess or host.

WONGREY'S COCKTAIL SAUCE

½ bottle ketchup [7 oz.]
1 T. Worcestershire sauce
½ T. powdered horseradish
1/8 t. Tabasco sauce
½ T. fresh or concentrated lemon juice

Mix ingredients thoroughly. Sauce can be served immediately or refrigerated for later use with boiled shrimp, steamed oysters, crabs, clams or raw oysters and clams.

REMOULADE SAUCE

This sauce is very versatile. It can include shrimp and be served as Shrimp Remoulade or Shrimp Remoulade Salad. You can omit the shrimp and use the sauce as a dip with boiled shrimp. The sauce also goes well with raw fresh vegetables such as carrot sticks, cauliflower, peeled cucumbers, sliced tomatoes or cherry tomatoes.

SHRIMP REMOULADE

¾ cup mayonnaise
½ cup boiled shrimp, chopped
2 hard-boiled eggs, chopped
1 t. salt
2 t. prepared mustard
6 green onions, finely minced
1 t. paprika
1 T. chopped parsley or parsley flakes
Dash Tabasco sauce

Mix ingredients, cover and refrigerate at least 3 hours before serving.

ONION DIP

This dip has become all but a staple item in America's kitchens. Usually served with potato chips and an assortment of cocktail crackers, this dip is also compatible with boiled shrimp.

1 8-oz. pkg. cream cheese
½ cup mayonnaise
½ T. grated onion

With electric mixer, whip cream cheese in mixing bowl until smooth. Blend in mayonnaise and onion. Chill and serve.

SOUR CREAM TARTAR SAUCE

Prepare as for Tartar Sauce (see Sauces to Accompany Fish), substituting ½ cup sour cream for mayonnaise.

CUCUMBER SAUCE

1 large cucumber, chopped fine or grated
½ cup mayonnaise [sour cream may be substituted]
½ T. lemon juice
½ t. salt
1/8 t. black pepper

Combine ingredients in bowl. Mix, chill and serve with boiled shrimp or freshly shucked oysters and clams. Also good with poached and fried seafoods.

HORSERADISH COCKTAIL SAUCE

1 cup ketchup
¼ cup chili sauce
Dash Tabasco sauce
Dash salt
Dash black pepper
1 t. lemon juice
1 t. prepared horseradish

Mix ingredients well, chill and serve with boiled shrimp, raw oysters, steamed oysters, raw clams, steamed clams and boiled crabs.

CHILI SAUCE

1 cup mayonnaise
½ cup chili sauce
1 t. lemon juice
Dash Worcestershire sauce
Dash Tabasco sauce

Mix well, chill and serve. Especially tasty on boiled shrimp.

DRAWN BUTTER

Melt ½ cup butter in saucepan. (You **must** use butter for this recipe.) Pour into transparent bowl and allow milk byproducts to settle to bottom. Pour back into saucepan, making sure sediment doesn't follow; reheat and serve either in a communal sauce bowl or individual butter dishes. Serve with boiled shrimp, raw oysters, steamed oysters, raw clams, steamed clams and boiled crabs.

For a Lemon Butter or Lime Butter, add 1 tablespoon lemon or lime juice to drawn butter when reheating. Other variations include the following: Omit lemon and lime juice and to each ½ cup drawn butter add either 1 teaspoon oregano, 1 teaspoon dill weed or 1 teaspoon prepared herb seasoning.

Still other variations include the addition of 1 tablespoon finely chopped spring onions or 1 tablespoon chopped pimiento to ½ cup drawn butter.

Part V

Salad Dressings and Salads

Salads are not only decorative, they are nutritious, quick and easy to prepare and inexpensive. Varied salad dressings make fish cookery, especially dishes containing crab meat and shrimp, a tantalizing avenue to eating adventure.

The following is certainly not an exhaustive list of salad dressings one can concoct, but we think they exemplify the basic types compatible with seafood dishes.

BLUE CHEESE DRESSING

1 3-oz. bar blue cheese
1 cup mayonnaise
1 T. lemon juice
Dash of paprika

Crumble cheese into bowl and fold in remaining ingredients. Do not whip, mash or beat. Chill.

THOUSAND ISLAND DRESSING

2 cups mayonnaise
1 cup chili sauce
1 T. dill pickle, chopped

Mix ingredients thoroughly. If you wish, you may add chopped white of 1 hard-boiled egg.

FRENCH DRESSING

½ **cup wine vinegar or lemon juice**
¼ **cup salad or olive oil**
1 t. powdered mustard
½ **t. salt**
Dash cayenne
1/8 t. black pepper
1 clove garlic

Place ingredients in jar, close and shake until ingredients are well blended. Refrigerate 2 to 3 hours. Remove garlic before serving.

VINAIGRETTE DRESSING

½ **cup olive oil**
1 T. white vinegar
½ **t. celery seed**
½ **t. salt**
1 t. Worcestershire sauce
1 clove garlic
Dash thyme

Place ingredients in jar, seal and shake to blend. Refrigerate at least 2 hours. Remove garlic and serve. (Note under Saltwater Fish that Vinaigrette Dressing is a delicious sauce for flounder.)

CUCUMBER DRESSING

We have already given this recipe as Cucumber Sauce. But it's just as suitable as a salad dressing.

JUST PLAIN LEMON DRESSING

Just Plain Lemon, as written, is sufficient for a salad dressing. Lemon juice adds that tartness so desired in fish salads. Lime can be used as a substitute, but we prefer the tangy lemon.

SALADS

CRAB SALAD

1 cup crab meat [shrimp can be substituted]
1 cup celery, diced
½ t. black pepper
½ t. salt
1 hard-boiled egg, diced
Juice of lemon or 1 T. concentrated lemon juice
2 cups shredded lettuce
½ cup mayonnaise

Combine all ingredients and toss gently. Serve at once. (**Do not refrigerate** after mixing. Refrigeration wilts lettuce which has been combined with mayonnaise and the salad become soggy.) Serves 4.

FISH SALAD

2 cups cooked, flaked fish
2 hard-boiled eggs, chopped
¼ cup mixed pickles, diced
½ cup mayonnaise
Salt and pepper to taste

Combine ingredients in mixing bowl and toss. Serve on lettuce leaves or shredded lettuce. Ring with freshly sliced tomatoes. Serves 4 to 6.

DEVILED EGGS WITH SHRIMP

12 boiled shrimp, chopped
4 hard-boiled eggs
1 T. pickle relish
1 T. prepared mustard
3 T. mayonnaise
½ t. salt
½ t. black pepper

Slice hard-boiled eggs in half, lengthwise, reserving the whites. Place yolks into mixing bowl and add relish, mustard, mayonnaise, salt and pepper. Blend on highest speed of mixer until smooth. Remove, fold in shrimp and stuff into boiled egg whites. Serve on bed of shredded lettuce. Serves 4.

SHRIMP SALAD

1 head shredded lettuce
1 cup boiled shrimp, halved
¼ cup mayonnaise
½ cup celery, chopped
Salt and pepper to taste

Place all ingredients into bowl and mix well. Serve on lettuce leaf bed and garnish with lemon wedges and black olives. Serves 4.

OYSTER SALAD

Drain liquor from raw oysters. Place oysters on bed of lettuce and squeeze lemon juice over them. Garnish with lemon wedges. (Allow 6 oysters per person.)

COMBINATION SALAD

1 head shredded lettuce
½ cup boiled shrimp, chopped
¼ cup crab meat
¼ cup cooked, flaked fish

Combine ingredients with shredded lettuce and toss. Divide into 4 salad bowls and top with either a Blue Cheese, Thousand Island, French or Vinaigrette dressing. Or you can toss lettuce with ¾ cup mayonnaise or ¾ cup fresh lemon juice.

STUFFED TOMATOES

4 large tomatoes
Shrimp, crab or fish

Follow directions for Shrimp Salad. Stuff tomatoes and serve to 4.

CRAB-MACARONI SALAD

1 cup crab meat [may substitute shrimp or flaked fish]
1 cup cooked macaroni
1 hard-boiled egg, chopped
¼ cup mayonnaise
1 T. dill pickle, chopped

Combine ingredients and serve to 4 on bed of lettuce leaves. Also complements stuffed tomatoes.

CRAB WITH OIL AND VINEGAR

1 cup crab meat [chopped boiled shrimp may be substituted]
1 head lettuce
½ cup celery, chopped
1 cucumber, peeled and diced
½ bell pepper, stripped
1 t. garlic salt
¼ cup vegetable or olive oil
1 T. wine vinegar

Wash lettuce, peel off outer leaves and break into bite-size portions. Add crab meat or shrimp, celery, cucumber and bell pepper. Sprinkle garlic salt over salad and toss. Add oil and vinegar and toss. Salt and pepper to taste. Serves 4.

NUTTY CRAB SALAD

See Crab salad. To this salad, add ½ cup chopped pecans.

SHRIMP AVOCADO BOATS

4 avocados
1 cup shrimp, chopped [flaked fish or crab meat may be substituted]
1 cup celery, diced
¼ cup mayonnaise
Lemon juice as required
Salt and pepper to taste

Halve avocados lengthwise without peeling. Scrape out pulp and discard. Sprinkle avocado halves with lemon juice to keep from turning brown. Place celery, shrimp, mayonnaise, salt and pepper in bowl and mix. Stuff mixture into avocado halves and serve to 4.

SHRIMP STICKS

This could be used as an hors d'oeuvre, but when mixed with shredded lettuce it also makes an excellent salad.

1 cup shrimp, diced
¼ cup mayonnaise
½ cup mild cheese, grated
½ T. pimiento, chopped
4 ribs celery, cut in 1-inch portions

In bowl, mix shrimp with mayonnaise, cheese and pimiento. Fill celery sticks. Shred 1 small head lettuce. Divide into serving bowls and add celery-shrimp sticks. Garnish with sweet onion rings.

CUCUMBER BOATS

4 cucumbers
1 cup shrimp, chopped
1 cup blue cheese dressing

Halve cucumbers lengthwise and scoop out pulp. Discard pulp. Mix shrimp and blue cheese dressing and stuff into cucumber halves. Serve to 4.

PEAR SALAD WITH SHRIMP

4 pear halves, canned
1 cup boiled shrimp, chopped
½ cup mayonnaise
1 T. pear syrup
½ cup mild cheese, grated

Mix mayonnaise and pear syrup together. Fold in shrimp. Stuff into pear halves and top with grated cheese. Serve on shredded lettuce to 4.

CRAB SALAD WITH PEAS

1 cup crab meat
¼ cup mayonnaise
½ cup celery, diced
2 hard-boiled eggs, chopped
½ cup canned sweet peas

Mix ingredients and serve on bed of lettuce leaves. Ring with sliced tomatoes, green olives and lemon wedges. Serves 4.

HOT SHRIMP SALAD WITH PECANS

1 cup boiled shrimp, chopped
1 cup celery, diced
¼ cup mayonnaise
½ cup sharp cheese, grated
½ t. onion juice
1 t. lemon juice
½ cup pecans, crushed

Mix ingredients and place in casserole dish. Cover with crushed pecans and bake 30 minutes at 350 degrees. Serves 4.

GREEN BEAN SALAD WITH SHRIMP

1 cup boiled shrimp, chopped
⅔ cup canned string beans
¼ cup carrots, grated
⅔ cup cabbage, shredded
2 T. bell pepper, chopped
4 T. mayonnaise

Combine ingredients and serve to 4.

SHRIMP WITH ONION DIP

1½ cups boiled shrimp, chopped

Prepare Onion Dip. (See Cocktail Sauces and Dips.) Add shrimp and stuff tomatoes, avocados or cucumber boats.

SLAW SALADS

The following dishes may also be prepared without seafood and served as a side dish with fish, but with the addition of either shrimp or crab meat, they become seafood salads.

A COLE SLAW SALAD FROM THE HOUSE OF WONGREY

1 head cabbage, shredded
2 t. sugar [or 1 t. sugar substitute]
1 t. salt
2 T. white vinegar
1 cup chopped shrimp [or 1 cup crab or fish meat]

Mix ingredients and serve to 4. You may garnish with tomato and lemon wedges.

HOLIDAY SLAW

4 cups cabbage, shredded
1 large unpeeled red apple, diced
½ t. salt
¾ cup mild cheddar cheese, cubed
½ cup mayonnaise
¼ t. Tabasco sauce
2 t. prepared mustard
2 cups chopped shrimp [or crab meat]

Combine cabbage, apple and salt. Add cheese cubes, mayonnaise, Tabasco, mustard and shrimp. Mix well. Cover and refrigerate 1 hour. Serve to 6.

HOT SLAW

1 head cabbage, shredded
1 medium onion, sliced thinly
1 cup shrimp or crab meat

Mix ingredients. In saucepan combine:

½ cup sugar [or ¼ cup sugar substitute]
½ cup white vinegar
¼ cup vegetable oil
½ T. celery seed
1 T. mustard seed

Bring to boil, reduce to simmer and cook 3 minutes. Pour over slaw, mix and serve to 4 to 6.

CABBAGE SLAW

1 cup boiled shrimp, chopped [or crab meat]
1 head cabbage, shredded
2 peeled carrots, grated
1 small onion, minced
1 T. pickle relish
½ cup mayonnaise

Mix ingredients and serve to 4.

ANOTHER SLAW FROM CABBAGE

1 cup boiled shrimp, chopped [or crab meat]
1 head cabbage, shredded
½ bell pepper, stripped
1 peeled red apple, diced
½ cup dark seedless raisins

Combine ingredients and toss with either Blue Cheese, Thousand Island or French Dressing. Serves 4 to 6.

RAISIN-CARROT SLAW

1 cup boiled shrimp, chopped [or crab meat]
4 medium carrots, grated
¼ t. salt
½ cup mayonnaise
½ cup dark seedless raisins

Toss ingredients and serve to 4 on bed of lettuce leaves.

POTATO SALADS

As with slaw salads, potato salads—when blended with shrimp or
crab meat—can either be served as an appetizer or as a dish with the
meal. You may exclude either the shrimp or crab meat and serve the
following dishes as an accompaniment to fish.

FIRST RECIPE

1 cup boiled shrimp, chopped [or crab meat]
4 medium potatoes
3 hard-boiled eggs
2 t. Worcestershire sauce
1½ t. salt
1 t. sweet pickle vinegar
½ cup mayonnaise
1 medium onion, minced

Place potatoes in pot, add 1 teaspoon salt and cover with water.
Bring to boil, reduce heat to medium and cook until fork can easily
be inserted into potatoes. Drain and let cool. Peel potatoes, dice and
place in mixing bowl with onion. Remove yolks from cooked eggs
and place into small bowl. Add Worcestershire, ½ teaspoon salt,
pickle vinegar and mayonnaise. Blend. Pour mixture over diced
potatoes and fold in shrimp and chopped egg whites. Serves 4 to 6.

SECOND RECIPE

2 cups boiled shrimp, chopped [or crab meat]
12 medium new potatoes, boiled
6 slices uncooked breakfast bacon, chopped
2 T. all-purpose flour
¼ cup white vinegar
1 cup water
1 t. celery seed
1 T. parsley flakes
3 hard-boiled eggs
Salt and pepper to taste

Boil potatoes in jackets, remove, peel and cut into chunks while hot.
Season potatoes with salt, pepper, celery seed and parsley. Toss
gently. Fry bacon, remove from pan and reserve 3 to 4 tablespoons
drippings. Stir in flour, vinegar and water and cook until thick. Add

shrimp, heat and pour over potatoes. Garnish with chopped egg and bacon. Serves 6 to 8.

THIRD RECIPE

1 cup boiled shrimp, chopped [or crab meat]
4 medium potatoes, boiled
1 t. salt
½ t. black pepper
1½ T. prepared mustard
1 T. mayonnaise

Cook potatoes and refrigerate 2 to 3 hours. Remove, peel and dice. Mix potatoes with remaining ingredients and serve on bed of lettuce. Garnish with tomato wedges. Serve to 4.

FOURTH RECIPE

1 cup boiled whole shrimp [or crab meat]
4 medium potatoes, boiled and diced
2 green onions with tops, chopped
1 t. salt
½ t. black pepper
1 cup sour cream

Mix ingredients well and serve to 4.

Part VI

Dishes to Accompany Fish

Fish or seafood is usually served with a green vegetable such as broccoli, spinach, asparagus, brussel sprouts, cabbage and string beans. But to restrict oneself to these dishes would limit both imagination and diversity.

Beets, cauliflower, onions, eggplant, tomatoes, squash and carrots are also vegetables which lend much to fish dishes.

Grits have long been a favorite below the Mason-Dixon Line and are more than at home with fried fish. And we certainly can't overlook our traditional rice and potato recipes.

BROCCOLI WITH BUTTER

1 8-oz. pkg. frozen broccoli, thawed
1 cup boiling water, seasoned with ½ t. salt.
1 T. melted butter or margarine

Place broccoli in boiling water. When water returns to boil, reduce to simmer, cover, and cook 4 to 6 minutes. Remove, drain, place in serving dish and pour melted butter over broccoli.

BROCCOLI WITH CHEESE SAUCE

Follow above directions, omit butter, and serve with Cheese Sauce when done. (See Cheese Sauce under Sauces to Accompany Fish.)

BROCCOLI WITH HOLLANDAISE

Follow directions for Broccoli with Butter but omit butter. Serve with Hollandaise. (See Sauces to Accompany Fish for Hollandaise Sauce.)

BROCCOLI WITH PARMESAN

Follow directions for Broccoli with Butter. Omit butter and lightly sprinkle grated Parmesan cheese over cooked broccoli.

All broccoli recipes given will serve 4 and accompany baked, broiled or poached fish.

TART SPINACH

1 15-oz. can spinach
1 freshly squeezed lemon or 1 T. concentrated lemon juice
1 t. lemon-and-pepper seasoning

Empty spinach into small pot; add lemon-and-pepper seasoning. Bring to slow boil. When spinach is hot, remove to serving dish, add lemon juice and serve. You may garnish with chopped fried bacon, hard-boiled egg wedges or grated egg yolks.

EASY CREAMED SPINACH

1 15-oz. can spinach
1 can condensed cream of chicken soup
1 soup can half-and-half

Empty spinach into small saucepan and heat slowly. Empty cream of chicken soup into another small pan, add a can of half-and-half and heat slowly. Drain liquid from spinach, add soup, stir and serve.

SPINACH WITH MUSHROOMS

1 15-oz. can spinach
1 2-oz. can mushroom stems and pieces

Empty spinach into saucepan. Drain liquid from mushrooms and add to spinach. Heat slowly and serve.

SPINACH WITH CROUTONS

1 15-oz. can spinach
2 slices white bread, cut in cubes
2 T. margarine or butter, melted

Empty spinach into saucepan. Heat slowly. While spinach is heating, sauté bread cubes in margarine or butter until brown. Remove, dust lightly with salt and paprika. Drain liquid from spinach, serve on individual plates and garnish with croutons.

The spinach recipes serve 4 and are adaptable to fried, broiled, baked or poached fish.

ASPARAGUS WITH HOLLANDAISE

1 1-lb., 3-oz. can asparagus

Empty asparagus with juice into saucepan and heat slowly. (Prepare Hollandaise Sauce as directed under Sauces to Accompany Fish.)

Drain liquid from asparagus, place on serving platter and pour Hollandaise over asparagus. For added color, garnish with either strips of pimiento or freshly chopped parsley.

ASPARAGUS VINAIGRETTE

1 1-lb., 3-oz. can asparagus

Heat asparagus slowly. (See recipe for Vinaigrette Dressing under Salad Dressings and Salads.) If prepared vinaigrette has been refrigerated, remove and heat slowly. Drain asparagus and serve with hot vinaigrette.

ASPARAGUS WITH HERB BUTTER

1 1-lb., 3-oz. can asparagus
¼ cup melted butter
1 t. prepared herb seasoning

Heat asparagus slowly. To prepare herb butter, in small saucepan melt butter. Pour into transparent bowl and allow milk byproducts in butter to settle to bottom. Pour back into saucepan, making sure sediment does not follow. Add herb seasoning and reheat. Drain asparagus and place in serving bowl. Pour herb butter over asparagus.

SAUTÉED ASPARAGUS

1 1-lb., 3-oz. can asparagus, drained
¼ cup margarine or butter

Melt margarine or butter in skillet over medium heat. Add asparagus, being careful not to break spears, and sauté slowly until asparagus is thoroughly heated. Remove gently to serving platter with pan juices. Add strips of pimiento for color.

The above recipes serve 4 and go well with baked, broiled, fried and poached fish.

RAW CUCUMBERS

Peel and slice cucumbers. Salt, pepper and serve. Excellent with fried fish.

FRIED CUCUMBERS

Peel and slice cucumbers. Salt, pepper and dust lightly with cracker or corn meal. Fry in hot vegetable oil until browned. Delicious with broiled fish.

CUCUMBERS IN VINAIGRETTE DRESSING

Peel and slice cucumbers. Place in serving bowl and add chilled Vinaigrette Dressing. (See recipe under Salad Dressings and Salads.) Fitting for fried, broiled or baked fish. You may substitute Blue Cheese, Thousand Island or French Dressing for vinaigrette.

CUCUMBERS WITH CHEESE SAUCE

Peel and slice 2 to 3 cucumbers. Lightly salt. No pepper. Place in serving bowl and add hot Cheese Sauce. (Under Sauces to Accompany Fish, see Cheese Sauce.) An appropriate dish for poached fish.

BRUSSEL SPROUTS WITH MELTED BUTTER

1 8-oz. pkg. frozen brussel sprouts, thawed
1 cup boiling water, seasoned with ½ t. salt
1 T. melted butter or margarine

Place brussel sprouts in boiling water. When water returns to boil, reduce to simmer, cover, and cook 4 to 6 minutes. Remove, drain, place in serving dish and pour melted butter over vegetables. You may omit butter and serve with either a Cheese or Hollandaise Sauce. Serves 4 and is tempting with baked, broiled or poached fish.

FRIED BRUSSEL SPROUTS

1 8-oz. pkg. frozen brussel sprouts, thawed
1½ T. margarine or butter
2 T. onion, chopped

Melt margarine in skillet over medium heat; add onion and lightly seasoned brussel sprouts with salt and pepper. Saute until sprouts have browned. Serves 4 and goes well with baked or broiled fish.

BOILED CABBAGE

1 head cabbage, cored and quartered
1 cup ham broth
Salt and pepper to taste

Bring broth to boil; add seasonings and cabbage. Allow to return to second boil, cover and cook until cabbage is tender but not mushy. (It requires only a few minutes. Cabbage should retain its pale green color.) Ideal for fried fish.

SAUTÉED CABBAGE

1 head cabbage, cored and shredded
2 T. margarine, butter or bacon drippings
Salt and pepper to taste

Melt margarine, butter or bacon drippings in skillet over medium heat. Add cabbage, seasonings and cook until cabbage is tender but firm. Serve with fried fish.

CABBAGE WITH CHEESE SAUCE

Prepare cabbage as for Boiled Cabbage. Prepare Cheese Sauce only moments before cabbage is done. (See recipe under Sauces to Accompany Fish.) Drain cabbage, place on serving platter and ladle with Cheese Sauce. Succulent with poached or broiled or baked fish.

STRING BEANS WITH TOMATOES

1 large onion, sliced into thin rings
1 cup ham broth
1 1-lb. can string beans, drained
1 1-lb. can whole tomatoes
1 T. vegetable oil

In 2-quart pot, sauté onions in oil on low heat until tender. Pour in ham broth. Add beans and tomatoes, salt and pepper to taste and cook on low heat until thoroughly heated. A must for baked or broiled fish.

BEANS WITH MUSHROOMS

1 1-lb. can string beans, drained
1 cup ham broth
1 2-oz. can mushroom stems and pieces, drained
Salt and pepper to taste

Combine ingredients in saucepan and heat slowly. Serves 4. A delicate blend of flavors for poached, broiled, baked or fried fish.

HERBED GREEN BEANS

1 1-lb. can string beans

Drain liquid from beans and heat in colander of double boiler. Prepare herb butter (see recipe under Asparagus with Herb Butter). Remove beans from colander, place in serving bowl and add herb butter. A pimiento garnish gives this dish a gourmet appearance. This dish gives a lift to fried, broiled, baked or poached fish.

PICKLED BEETS

1 1-lb. can small whole beets
1 medium onion, sliced
1 t. sugar [½ t. sugar substitute]
1 t. salt
2 T. white vinegar

Empty beets with liquid into bowl. Add remaining ingredients and toss lightly. Refrigerate at least a half hour. Gives both color and zest to fried, broiled or baked fish.

HARVARD BEETS

1 1-lb. can small whole beets
¼ cup white vinegar
1 T. sugar [½ T. sugar substitute]
1½ T. cornstarch

Drain beet juice into saucepan. Bring to slow boil; add cornstarch and thicken to medium sauce. Add vinegar, beets and sugar and stir until beets have heated. Pour into serving bowl and garnish with fresh parsley. Suitable for baked or broiled fish.

CAULIFLOWER WITH HOLLANDAISE

1 8-oz. pkg. frozen cauliflower, thawed
1 cup boiling water, seasoned with ½ t. salt

Place cauliflower in boiled water. When water returns to boil, reduce to simmer, cover, and cook 4 to 6 minutes. Remove, drain, place in serving dish and top with Hollandaise Sauce. (See Sauces to Accompany Fish.) Serves 4 with either poached, broiled or baked fish.

If you prefer a Cheese Sauce, this recipe can be found under Sauces to Accompany Fish.

CAULIFLOWER WITH LEMON BUTTER

1 8-oz. pkg. frozen cauliflower, thawed
1 cup boiling water, seasoned with ½ t. salt

Prepare cauliflower as for Cauliflower with Hollandaise. In another saucepan add:

¼ cup margarine or butter
1 T. fresh lemon or concentrated lemon juice
1 t. parsley flakes

Heat. Remove cauliflower from water and into serving dish. Pour lemon butter over top and serve to 4. Both colorful and light when served with fried, broiled, poached or baked fish.

CREAMED WHOLE ONIONS

1 1-lb. can whole onions
1 cup onion liquid
2 T. margarine or butter
2 T. all-purpose flour
1 cup sweet milk
Salt and pepper to taste

Melt margarine in saucepan. Add flour and stir to smooth paste. Stir in onion juice. Add milk, gradually, for desired thickness. Fold in onions, salt and pepper and stir until onions are heated. Remove to serving dish. You may wish to garnish with paprika. An excellent accompaniment for fried, broiled, baked or poached fish.

FRIED ONION RINGS

Onions cooked in this manner are best fried in a deep-fat fryer; however, a skillet or electric fry pan will suffice.

3 medium Spanish onions, peeled and sliced about ¼ inch thick
1 egg
2 cups milk
Flour as required
Cracker or corn meal as required

Separate onion slices into rings and flour. Beat egg lightly, add milk and whip again. Dip onion rings into egg-milk mixture and dust lightly with cracker or corn meal. Place in preheated skillet (375 degrees for electric fry pan) containing about an inch of oil. Fry until rings are golden.

FRIED EGGPLANT

Peel and slice eggplant in circular slices. If eggplant is large, halve slices. Salt and pepper and follow directions for preparing Fried Onion Rings. A treat when served with broiled or baked fish.

FRIED GREEN TOMATOES

Prepare as for Fried Cucumbers. An unusual accompaniment for broiled fish.

TOMATOES PROVENCALE

4 fresh ripe tomatoes
¾ cup soft bread crumbs
1½ T. chopped parsley or parsley flakes
1 clove garlic, crushed
Olive oil as required
Salt and pepper to taste

Preheat oven to 425 degrees and lightly grease a shallow baking pan. Slice tomatoes in halves and place in pan. Season cut tops with salt and pepper. Combine bread crumbs, parsley and garlic and spread on top of tomatoes. Sprinkle with oilve oil. Bake until bread crumbs have lightly browned—about 15 minutes. Serve 1 tomato half per person with broiled, baked or poached fish.

BROILED TOMATOES

4 ripe tomatoes, halved
¼ cup melted margarine or butter
Salt and pepper to taste

Place tomatoes in pie pan; baste with margarine and salt and pepper. Place under preheated broiler 4 inches from coils for about 5 minutes. Garnish with parsley and serve with broiled or baked fish.

SQUASH WITH HAM BROTH

Like cabbage, we Southerners rarely steam squash but prefer to cook them in ham broth.

8 squash
½ cup ham broth
Salt and pepper to taste

Wash and slice squash in circular slices. Place in pot with ham broth. Add no water. Salt and pepper to taste. Bring to slow boil, reduce heat to simmer, cover and cook until tender, but not mushy.

Only a few minutes' cooking time required. Serve to 4 with fried, baked, broiled or poached fish.

LOIS'S (MRS. JAN WONGREY'S) SKILLET FRIED SQUASH

8 yellow squash, sliced circular
1 onion, chopped
2 T. bacon drippings
Salt and pepper to taste

In skillet, on medium heat, add seasoned squash and onions to hot bacon drippings. Stir gently as squash begins to cook for 3 to 4 minutes. Reduce to low heat, cover, and cook until squash are tender but retain their texture. Most appetizing with either fried or broiled fish.

SQUASH CASSEROLE

4 - 5 yellow crooked neck squash
½ cup sour cream
2 egg whites
3 strips cooked bacon, crumbled
¼ cup pimiento, chopped
1 cup toasted bread crumbs mixed with 1 T. melted margarine
1 2-oz. can sliced mushrooms

Scrub whole squash, place in boiling water (no salt) and cook until fork can easily be inserted—about 3 minutes. Remove, drain and slice ¼ inch thick. Salt and pepper each side lightly. Layer bottom of baking dish with squash. Separate egg whites from yolks. Beat whites slightly with fork, fold in sour cream and frost squash. Sprinkle bacon and pimiento over first layer. Repeat layers until squash are used. Sprinkle top with bread crumbs, and garnish with mushrooms. Place dish into preheated 400 degree oven and cook 30 minutes. Delectable with fried, baked, broiled or poached fish.

BUTTERED CARROTS

This vegetable cooked in the simplest manner is perhaps the most ideal of all vegetables to serve with fried, broiled, baked or poached fish.

6 medium carrots, cut in circular slices
1 cup water
1 t. salt
1 T. margarine or butter, melted

Peel carrots and place in pot with salt and water. Bring to a boil, cover, reduce to low heat and cook until fork can be inserted. Remove, drain and place into serving bowl. Pour melted margarine or butter over carrots. You may garnish with fresh parsley or dried parsley flakes.

CARROTS AND PEAS

2 cups cooked carrots
1 cup canned garden peas

Combine peas and carrots in pot and heat. Serve with fried, baked, broiled or poached fish.

SOUTHERN GRITS

This dish, sometimes served with milk and sugar to the north, is as at home with fried fish as it is with 2 eggs sunnyside-up, country ham and biscuits.

2½ cups water
1 t. salt
1 cup grits
1 T. margarine or butter, melted

Bring water to boil, add grits and salt and stir until water returns to second boil. Reduce heat to simmer, cover and cook until water is absorbed by grits. When done, pour into serving bowl and add margarine or butter. Serve with fried fish or stews.

HERBED RICE

2½ cups chicken broth
1 cup uncooked, long grain rice
3 T. margarine or butter
2 T. dried chives, chopped
¼ t. basil
¼ t. savory
¼ t. garlic salt

Bring chicken broth to boil; stir in rice, cover, reduce to simmer and cook until done—30 minutes. While rice is cooking, melt margarine in saucepan, add herbs and garlic salt, stir and heat. Remove cooked rice to serving bowl and mix in seasoned margarine. Serves 4 to 6 persons with either fried, baked, broiled or poached fish.

MUSHROOM RICE

2 cups uncooked, long grain rice
1 can beef bouillon
1 can beef consommé
1 2-oz. can mushroom stems and pieces
½ stick margarine or butter
1 medium onion, chopped

Place ingredients in 2-quart casserole dish, cover and bake at 400 degrees until done—1 hour. Superb with baked, broiled, or poached fish. Serves 4 to 6.

RICE WITH PARSLEY

1 cup uncooked, long grain rice
2½ cups water, seasoned with 1 t. salt
1 t. margarine or butter
1 t. parsley flakes

Bring water to boil, add rice, stir until second boil. Reduce heat to simmer, cover and cook until done (about 30 minutes). When rice is cooked, add margarine and parsley flakes. Serve to 4. A treat with fried, baked, broiled or poached fish.

FRIED RICE

2 cups cooked, long grain rice [refrigerated at least 24 hours]
¼ cup vegetable oil
2 eggs, beaten
2 spring onions with tops, chopped
2½ T. soy sauce

In skillet, over medium heat, heat cooking oil; add rice and sauté until rice browns. Stir in eggs, cook and add soy sauce. Remove to serving dish and top with chopped onions and tops. Unmatched with broiled, baked or poached fish. Serves 4 to 6.

FRIED POTATOES

Peel potatoes, halve and slice into what are known as "shoe-strings." After slicing, place in pan or bowl of water to keep them from turning brown. In skillet or electric fry pan, place potatoes in preheated vegetable oil at least 1 inch deep. Fry until potatoes have bowned. Excellent with fried fish.

SKILLET FRIED POTATOES

Peel 4 potatoes, halve and slice in ¾ inch thickness. Salt and pepper to taste and place in skillet with preheated vegetable oil and 1 sliced onion. Keep on medium heat, stirring, until potatoes are browned and crunchy. Serve with fried fish.

BOILED POTATOES

Wash, but do not peel, 8 to 10 new potatoes. Place in pot, cover with water and add 1 teaspoon salt. Bring to boil, reduce to low and cook until fork can be inserted. Remove and halve so that portions are held together by the skin on one side. Place in serving dish, dot with melted margarine or butter and garnish with parsley flakes. Most fitting served with fried, baked, broiled or poached fish.

SCALLOPED POTATOES

6 medium potatoes
Salt and pepper to taste
Flour as required
Milk as required

Peel and thinly slice potatoes. Salt, pepper and flour each slice lightly and layer in buttered casserole dish. Barely cover with milk. Repeat process until potatoes are consumed. Cover dish and place into 350 degree preheated oven. Cook for 1½ hours. Uncover last 15 to 20 minutes to brown. Potatoes should easily pierce with fork when done. A pleasant dish to accompany broiled or baked fish. Serves 4 to 6.

BAKED POTATOES WITH ONIONS

Scrub hard 4 nice baking potatoes and thinly slice 1 medium onion. Rub each potato lightly with vegetable oil; place individually on aluminum foil. Divide sliced onions among potatoes and wrap. Place in pan in oven preheated to 400 degrees and bake 40 to 45 minutes or until potatoes give when pressed with thumb and index finger. Serve with baked or broiled fish.

POTATOES WITH CHEESE SAUCE

In water seasoned with 1 teaspoon salt, add 8 to 10 peeled whole new potatoes. When water comes to boil, reduce to low heat, cover and cook until done.

Just before potatoes are ready, prepare Cheese Sauce. (See Sauces to Accompany Fish.) Remove potatoes from pot, place in serving bowl and top with Cheese Sauce. A must for baked, broiled or poached fish.

Part VII

Outdoor Cookery

Bill Cockerill, a tall, lean fellow with a Cherokee Indian face, skinned four sweet onions, diced them up and dropped them in a kettle with a half-pound of streak o' lean. The cooking meat, sliced longways, browned and curled over the hot fire. Fresh onions popped in the grease. The aroma was enticing.

A dozen bluish-black bream were scaled, cleaned, washed, salt and peppered and placed on a brown grocery sack. Bill layered them in the black cooking kettle, covered them with onions and added Tabasco and Worcestershire sauce. He topped the mixture with ketchup and the fried meat. The process was repeated until the fish were consumed. A pot of water was put on for rice. The skillet, greased by the fried meat, was used to cook cornbread pancakes.

We were deep in South Carolina's Santee Swamp. Bream were bedding and slapping everything that hit the water, and it didn't take long to find a bed. Supple canepoles were bent, line zig-zagged through the water, two cricket boxes were emptied and we had a grand time while the bream raised a ruckus. The air was cool and trees were sporting a fresh outfit of green.

There is a booming market today in canned scents. With a push of a button you can have assorted fruit and flower fragrances. But no one has yet come up with one that works on the olfactory system like that of a fish stew wafting on a gentle river breeze when the sun settles for the night in a musky cypress swamp.

We worked our way down past the second layer of fish and two skillets of bread. Fireflies danced and bullfrogs bellowed as night deepened. We sat near the open fire and sopped our plates clean with the last of the cornbread. It was fish eating at its finest.

It has been our pleasure to become acquainted with many river-bank cooks; we've enjoyed both their company and culinary delights which were prepared with the simplest of cooking implements and ingredients: streak o' lean, onions, salt, pepper and corn meal. But even this is overshadowed by their knowledge of how to cook fish over a bed of embers without burning or drying the fish, or soaking them in oil. Now we wish we had paid more attention to their lessons. We were too busy eating when we should have been observing and listening.

While we've cooked our share of fish over a bed of coals, we've never been able to repeat this process with exactness. Too often the coals are too hot or too cool. But we know with assurance that hickory or oak is superior to the other woods for cooking purposes. Pine will suffice if nothing else is at hand, but pine not only burns rapidly, it also smokes excessively.

The outdoor cook who has problems getting the cooking oil to the proper temperature has an alternate friend in the form of aluminum foil. Fish, especially largemouth bass, are a more-than-welcome sight at day's end when prepared in this manner.

Though we're quite fond of food cooked over hardwood coals, outdoor cookery is far easier on a charcoal grill.

Preparing The Grill:

(1) Cover the grill with perforated alumnium foil before cooking. This not only helps keep the grill clean, but also does not allow fish to fall through while cooking. Foil also eliminates sticking.

(2) Place charcoal in a pyramid stack, douse with liquid charcoal starter, wait five to six minutes and light. When charcoal turns ash grey, spread evenly. (You can presoak charcoal with liquid starter in an empty can prior to using. But remember to stack in a pyramid before starting.)

(3) Start the fire thirty to forty minutes before grilling. There should be no flames when you begin to cook.

(4) To reduce heat, raise the grill or spread coals.

(5) To increase heat, lower the grill or bring the coals closer together.

(6) Cook fish five inches from coals. When fish begin to flake with fork, gently remove with spatula to keep fish from falling apart.

BARBEQUE SAUCES

Outdoor cooks take great pride in concocting barbeque sauces. We have assembled a few for you to try on your own home grill.

FIRST SAUCE

1 cup white vinegar
1 cup ketchup
1 T. prepared mustard

Heat vinegar. Stir in ketchup and mustard and continue heating slowly, about 10 minutes.

SECOND SAUCE

2 cups white vinegar
1 t. cayenne

Mix together and heat slowly, about 10 minutes.

THIRD SAUCE

½ cup sweet pickle, chopped
½ cup onion, chopped
1 cup ketchup
1 T. prepared mustard
1 T. sweet pickle juice
Dash Tabasco
Dash Worcestershire

Sauté onions and pickle in ¼ cup water until tender. Drain excess water, add ketchup, mustard, pickle juice, Tabasco and Worcestershire. Heat slowly, about 10 minutes.

FOURTH SAUCE

2 T. margarine or butter
1 t. onion flakes
1/8 t. garlic salt
1/8 t. celery salt
1 cup ketchup

Melt margarine in saucepan, add ketchup and heat slowly. Add onion flakes, garlic salt and celery salt. Heat slowly, about 10 minutes.

FIFTH SAUCE

In saucepan heat:

1 cup ketchup
1 cup water
¼ cup white vinegar
2 t. Worcestershire sauce
2 t. prepared mustard
1 t. salt
1 garlic clove

Heat ingredients about 10 mintes. Remove garlic upon removal of sauce from stove.

SIXTH SAUCE

1 cup white vinegar
¼ cup prepared mustard

Heat together slowly, about 10 minutes.

The above barbeque sauces can be used to baste your favorite fish, whether whole, steaked or filleted. Remember to line the grill with foil, have an even distribution of coals and cook five inches from coals until fish begins to flake.

OYSTERS AND CLAMS

Scrub free of mud and place on perforated aluminum foil over coals. The heat will cause shellfish to open. Cook 5 inches from heat. Have ready your favorite cocktail sauce or dip.

SHRIMP

Ideal for the grill when cooked shish kabob fashion. No aluminum foil needed, just place skewers 5 inches from heat. Our favorite method is to alternate shrimp with whole button mushrooms, cherry tomatoes and sweet bermuda onions, and brush with any of the above barbeque sauces.

BASS BAKED IN ALUMINUM FOIL

Scale and clean fish. Salt and pepper inside and out. Place several thin slices of onion into cavity and 1 tablespoon margarine or butter. Wrap fish in foil, secure loose ends and the fold, place into coals and cover with bed of coals. Fish should be done in no less than 20 to 25 minutes.

Part VIII

Breads and Stuffings

A meal of fried fish or fish stew wouldn't be complete if it were not accompanied by hushpuppies. In the event you haven't heard the story of how the hushpuppy got its name, we will relate it. We do not know the family or place where this most historic moment in history took place, but it allegedly occured on a Deep South plantation.

Deer hounds were indigenous to the southern plantation scene and their puppies were as prized as cotton and rice crops. Meals were often served on the grounds when the weather allowed such dining conditions and the puppies were turned out from their kennels to eat hardily and happily from table scraps tossed to the ground.

On one such occasion the puppies were apparently not satisfied by the table offerings provided. In an attempt to appease the yapping puppies the owner tossed several "corn biscuits," as they were called, to the ground yelling, "Hush puppies!" The yapping ceased and was followed with whimpers of satisfaction. The corn biscuits were instantly dubbed "hushpuppies."

HUSHPUPPIES

2 cups corn meal
1 t. salt
1 t. sugar [½ t. sugar substitute]
2 t. baking powder
1½ T. fresh onion, minced
2 eggs, beaten
½ cup sweet milk

Place corn meal, salt, sugar, baking powder and onions into mixing bowl and blend ingredients together. Fold in eggs, milk and continue mixing. Preheat skillet or electric fry pan with vegetable oil about 1 inch deep. When oil comes to a bubble, drop 1 spoonful of batter at a time into oil. Reduce heat to medium and cook until browned. Drain on paper towels and serve with fried or stewed fish—in particular a catfish stew.

SCRATCH CORNBREAD

2 cups plain yellow corn meal
3 t. baking powder
1 egg
1½ cups sweet milk
3 T. vegetable oil or bacon drippings
1 t. salt

Combine eggs, milk and vegetable oil. Add remaining ingredients and stir until smooth. Dot muffin pan with vegetable oil or bacon drippings. Preheat pan or pans in oven about 3 minutes, remove and pour in the batter—about ⅔ full. Place in oven preheated to 425 degrees and bake 20 to 25 minutes.

As a variation, you can pour mixture into greased, preheated 9-inch pie pan and bake. Or you can pour batter into greased, preheated corn stick molds and bake.

CORNBREAD FROM CORNBREAD MIX

Prepare as directed on wrapper. However, we have found in using such mixes that if we add 2 eggs instead of 1, plus 1 teaspoon vegetable oil or bacon drippings, we achieve a richer, better-textured bread.

CHEESE CORNBREAD

Add ½ cup grated cheese to batter prepared from corn meal, as for Scratch Cornbread, or from package mixes.

PANCAKE CORNBREAD

1 cup all-purpose flour
1 cup corn meal
1 whole egg
1 cup sweet milk

Mix ingredients together. Using a ¼ cup measure, drop batter in lightly greased skillet. Turn once and cook until brown.

BISCUITS

2 cups all-purpose flour
3 t. baking powder
1 t. salt
⅓ cup shortening
¾ cup sweet or buttermilk

Empty flour into sifter. Add baking powder and salt and sift into mixing bowl. Add ⅓ cup shortening. Knead flour and shortening with hands until lumps and small beads are removed. Batter should now be workable but not sticky. Add milk and mix with hands. Remove and place on lightly floured table. Do not roll with rolling pin. Pinch off a handful of dough and flatten with hand. Cut with biscuit cutter, or make-do with an empty orange juice can or a small jelly glass. Place on lightly greased baking sheet and bake in oven preheated to 450 degrees until biscuits rise and lightly brown.

MAYONNAISE BISCUITS

2 cups all-purpose flour
½ cup mayonnaise
½ cup sweet milk

Mix ingredients and drop spoonfuls onto ungreased baking sheet. Bake at 450 degrees until biscuits brown.

STUFFINGS

Those rice dishes previously mentioned in Dishes to Accompany Fish, are excellent stuffings. Rice dishes should be cooked, cooled and refrigerated before using as a stuffing.

SHRIMP STUFFING

Use for 2- to 2½-lb. fish

> ½ lb. boiled shrimp
> 1 T. vegetable oil
> 1 medium onion, chopped
> 1 bell pepper, halved and chopped

Sauté onion, pepper in oil until tender. Remove, place in bowl and add:

> 1 egg
> ½ t. Tabasco sauce
> 1 t. Worcestershire sauce
> 10 saltine crackers, rolled fine

Mix ingredients, fold in shrimp and stuff your favorite fish. (One cup of flaked fish or crab meat may be substituted for shrimp.)

BREAD STUFFING

Use for 2- to 2½-lb. fish

> 3 cups very lightly toasted bread cubes
> ½ cup celery, thinly sliced
> ¼ cup onion, chopped
> 4 T. margarine or butter
> 1 t. salt
> 1 t. dill weed

Sauté celery and onion in margarine until tender. Remove, place in bowl and combine with remaining ingredients.

CLAM DRESSING

Use for 4- to 5-lb. fish

> 2 cups cooked cornbread, crumbled
> 1 cup clams with liquor
> 1 T. melted margarine or butter

Mince clams, add to cornbread and mix. Add clam liquor and margarine and combine. (Oysters can be substituted for clams.)

CRAB STUFFING

Use for 2- to 3-lb. fish

½ cup crab meat
1 cup cracker crumbs
2 T. margarine or butter
½ t. dill weed
½ t. oregano
¼ cup sherry

Sauté dill weed and oregano in melted margarine 3 to 4 minutes. Add crab meat and sauté 2 minutes. Remove, pour in bowl and stir in cracker crumbs. Add sherry.

POTATO STUFFING

Use for 2½- to 3-lb. fish

4 medium potatoes, peeled, boiled and chopped fine
1 onion, finely chopped
1 T. lemon juice
1 t. salt
½ t. pepper
½ t. prepared herb seasoning
2 T. melted margarine or butter

Combine potatoes and onion in bowl. Add lemon juice, salt, pepper and herb seasoning and mix well. Add margarine and blend.

Part IX

Cleaning and Freezing Fish

The fresher the fish the better. We cannot emphasize too much this most important point concerning fish cookery. Decay begins the moment a fish ceases floundering.

We know that it is next to impossible, and for some fishermen impossible, to cease fishing when fish are biting. This isn't to say that you should catch a fish, clean it and return to fishing. But it is important to ice fish down immediately upon retrieving them from the water.

If there is a lull, you could use this time to clean or begin to clean your catch.

Empty bread wrappers, plastic bags or freezer bags are excellent containers in which to keep cleaned fish. Remember to seal the bag or bags before placing on ice to prevent water from sogging the meat and impairing the flavor.

CLEANING FISH

Scaling

Manufactured scalers can be purchased, but if caught in a pinch, a pocket knife, spoon or fork will suffice. We're personally not too fond of scaling with a fork as it has a tendency to tear the meat.

Holding the head of the fish, start at the tail and scale back toward the head; take care not to stick your hand with a spine. After the fish is scaled, both sides, remove the head. Then slit the stomach with a knife, remove the entrails and wash.

You may notice that we gave no directions as to removal of the tail and dorsal fin. While some fishermen sever these fins during the cleaning process, we leave them since we find the fins a delicacy when fried crunchy. We're referring, of course, to the fins of pan-fish, largemouths and freshwater trout.

Skinning

This method of cleaning is used in the preparation of catfish. Cut the skin completely around the body just below the head and pectoral fins. Work it loose so you can grip it with pliers. Take hold of the skin with pliers in one hand, hold the head with the other and strip down to the tail. After removing the skin, split the fish down the stomach and clean. Removal of the tail is optional as it is tasty when fried and adds flavor to catfish stews.

Filleting

We like to fillet fish because it's quick and less messy. Two things are needed to fillet: a sharp knife and a flat surface. A small cutting board is ideal, but a large boat paddle or the top of an ice cooler will do.

To fillet, place the fish on its side and make a cut behind the gills. The incision should go no further than the backbone. When this is done, work the knife along the back down to the tail, leaving the backbone intact. Lift meat. Repeat for other side.

Place the fillet on the board and carefully slide the knife between the meat and skin. It is important to keep a firm hold on the skin as you cut; otherwise you will end up with scraps of meat. Keep sliding the knife—do not cut—until meat and skin are separated. The blade should be kept at a flat rather than a cutting angle.

Those who prefer to have the skin left on fish scale the fish before filleting them.

Butterfly Filleting

This type of cut is not hard to master and is recommended for jackfish. Butterfly fillets are simply the fillets held together by the unservered belly skin of a fish.

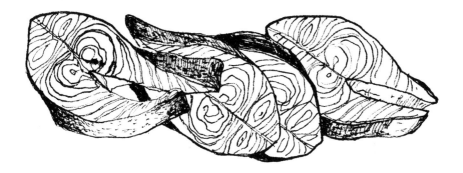

Fillet as above, taking care to leave the belly skin intact. (This forms a hinge between the two fillets.) Of course, you must scale the fish first. Butterly fillets do not require the removal of the fish skin.

Steaking

Steaks are center cut cross-sections of large dressed fish. Lay the fish on its side and cut through it. Most people prefer fish steaks at least an inch thick.

King mackerel, cobia and sharks are ideal for this method of preparation.

Fish Sticks

Follow directions for filleting, then remove skin. Place meat on a board and cross-cut into widths of one-half inch.

FREEZING FISH

One of our favorite methods of freezing fish is accomplished with the use of a milk carton. This is especially favored when filleting panfish such as bream, redbreasts, small white bass and small crappies.

Place fillets into a washed milk carton and fill with water until it just covers the layered fish. Close carton flap and freeze. Next time you have another successful catch, prepare the fish for freezing, bring out the milk carton from the freezer and repeat the above procedure.

Plastic containers are also useful for freezing fish.

Large whole, cleaned fish, large fillets and steaks should be frozen in freezer paper. You should keep in mind when wrapping fish for the freezer not to freeze more fish in a package than you think you will prepare for a given meal. **Do not try to refreeze fish once they have been thawed.**

Fish and shellfish will not keep indefinitely in a freezer. The following is a guide to the storage of frozen fish. Storing longer than recommended periods will result in impairment of flavor.

Lean fish (Largemouth bass and most freshwater fish)—4 to 6 months

Fatty fish (bluefish, Spanish mackerel), clams, oysters, raw shrimp—3 to 4 months

Cooked crabmeat—2 to 3 months

Cooked shrimp—1 to 2 months

FREEZING SHELLFISH

Since we have already discussed the cleaning of shrimp, crabs, clams and oysters, we will not repeat this information. However, remember that clams and oysters should be frozen in their liquor to retain flavor.

When preparing clams and oysters for freezing, you should work over a cheesecloth placed over a bowl. This cloth will catch grit, but will allow natural juices to strain through into the bowl. Place shucked clams or oysters in a plastic container, cover with juices and freeze.

Crab meat freezes well in plastic freezer bags as does shrimp— green or boiled.

THAWING

Fish should be thawed on a drain board of some type to accommodate dripping. If allowed to thaw in the melt, fish not only lose flavor but the meat becomes soggy.

Thawing fillets is easy: Place fillets into a colander and thaw in the sink.

ELIMINATING THE ODOR

Fish either cleaned in the home or cooked in the home, especially fried fish, leave a distinct and unpleasant odor.

The cleaner can rinse his hands in either lemon juice or white vinegar when through cleaning to help eliminate the fishy smell.

The cook can leave small open jars of white vinegar in out-of-sight places in the kitchen. It is also a good idea to operate the range hood fan while cooking fish. This will at least vacuum away cooking fumes.

FISH PURCHASING TIPS

Okay, so you don't fish, but enjoy eating them. Luckily, most towns have one or more good seafood markets. Follow these basic rules when purchasing:

(1) Eyes of fish should be clear and sparkling.
(2) Gills should be a reddish pink and absent of odor. If there is the slightest odor other than natural fish smell—**reject.**
(3) Scales should be free of slime and in full color.
(4) Flesh should be textured and springy when pressed.

Index

140

NOTES

NOTES

NOTES

Other Books Available From The Sandlapper Store, Inc.

The Sandlapper Store, Inc., has acquired the book publishing business of Sandlapper Press, Inc. and has all the titles published by Sandlapper Press Inc.

BATTLEGROUND OF FREEDOM
South Carolina In The Revolution.
By Nat and Sam Hilborn $12.95

FROM STOLNOY TO SPARTANBURG,
The Two Worlds of a Former Russian Princess.
By Marie Gagarine. $3.95

THE GREEN DRAGOON,
The Lives of Banastre Tarleton and Mary Robinson.
By Robert D. Bass. $6.95

LAUGH WITH THE JUDGE,
Humorous Anecdotes from a Career on the Bench.
By Bruce Littlejohn, Associate Justice,
the Supreme Court of South Carolina. $6.95

THE PENDLETON LEGACY,
An Illustrated History of the District
By Beth Ann Klosky $7.50

A PIECE OF THE FOX'S HIDE.
By Katharine Boling. $8.50

THE SANDLAPPER COOKBOOK
Compiled by Catha W. Reid and Joseph T. Bruce, Jr. $5.95

THE SOUTH CAROLINA DISPENSARY,
A Bottle Collector's Atlas and History of the System
By Phillip Kenneth Huggins. $5.95

Prices subject to change.
Add 75¢ per book for mailing and handling.
S.C. residents add 4% sales tax to the cost of the books.

THE COLUMBIA SAILING CLUB COOKBOOK
By The Ladies Auxiliary $5.95

HOG HEAVEN
A Guide to S.C. Barbecue
By Patricia Allie Wall and Ron L. Layne $3.95
Illustrated by Diane Wise Lay

CHILDREN'S BOOKS

ADVENTURES IN SOUTH CAROLINA,
An Educational Coloring Book.
Written by Linda Hirschmann.
Drawings by Sharon Applebaum   **$1**.75

THE MYSTER OF THE PIRATE'S TREASURE
By Idella Bodie.
Illustrated by Louise Yancey $3.95

THE SECRET OF TELFAIR INN.
Written by Idella Bodie.
Illustrations by Louise Yancey $3.95

SURGEON, TRADER, INDIAN CHIEF.
Henry Woodward of Carolina
By William O. Steele.
Illustrated by Hoyt Simmons $1.50

TURNING THE WORLD UPSIDE DOWN
By William and Patricia Willimon. $1.50

THE WHANG DOODLE,
Folk Tales from the Carolinas
Edited by Jean Cothran
Illustrated by Nance Studio. $3.95

GHOST IN THE CAPITOL
By Idella Bodie
Illustrated by Mary Arnold Garvin $3.95

SOUTH CAROLINA: A SYNOPTIC HISTORY FOR LAYMEN
By Lewis P. Jones. Paperback $7.95

WIND FROM THE MAIN,
A Novel by Anne Osborne $2.50

PLUM TREE LANE
By Lodwick Hartley $9.95

S.C. WOMEN: They Dared to Lead
By Idella F. Bodie $9.95

CARBINE: The Story of David Marshall Williams
By Ross E. Beard, Jr. $12.50

THE EXECUTION OF ISAAC HAYNE
By David Bowden $9.95

A CONTEMPLATIVE FISHING GUIDE TO THE GRAND STRAND
By Donald Millus $2.95

NINETY SIX
The Struggle for the S.C. Back Country
By Robert D. Bass $12.50

SWAMP FOX
By Robert D. Bass $7.50

S.C.'S CIVIL WAR OF 1775
By Lewis F. Jones $3.95

HOME BY THE RIVER
By Archibald Rutledge $10.00

SAGA OF AN EGO TRIP
By Jeannette Durlach $1.95
Illustrated by Marcus Durlach

WHAT THE WIND FORGETS
By Helen von Kolnitz Hyer $7.95
Poet Laureate of S.C.

SOUTHERN WILDFOWL AND WILD GAME COOKBOOK
By Jan Wongrey $4.95
Illustrated by Laura Peck

TO: THE SANDLAPPER STORE, INC.
      P.O. Box 841
      Lexington, South Carolina 29072

Please send me_____ copies of the **Southern Fish and Seafood Cookbook**
at $4.95* per copy plus 75¢ per copy (for postage and handling). Orders for 5 or
more books postpaid. S.C. residents add 4% sales tax to the cost of the books.

Name _____

Street _____

City _____

State & Zip_____

* price subject to change

- -

TO: THE SANDLAPPER STORE, INC.
      P.O. Box 841
      Lexington, South Carolina 29072

Please send me _____ copies of the **Southern Fish and Seafood Cookbook**
at $4.95* per copy plus 75¢ per copy (for postage and handling). Orders for 5 or
more books postpaid. S.C. residents add 4% sales tax to the cost of the books.

Name _____

Street _____

City _____

State & Zip_____

* price subject to change

- -

TO: THE SANDLAPPER STORE, INC.
      P.O. Box 841
      Lexington, South Carolina 29072

Please send me _____ copies of the **Southern Fish and Seafood Cookbook**
at $4.95* per copy plus 75¢ per copy (for postage and handling). Orders for 5 or
more books postpaid. S.C. residents add 4% sales tax to the cost of the books.

Name _____

Street _____

City _____

State & Zip_____

* price subject to change

TO: THE SANDLAPPER STORE, INC.
P.O. Box 841
Lexington, South Carolina 29072

Please send me _____ copies of the **Southern Fish and Seafood Cookbook** at $4.95* per copy plus 75¢ per copy (for postage and handling). Orders for 5 or more books postpaid. S.C. residents add 4% sales tax to the cost of the books.

Name _____

Street _____

City _____

State & Zip_____

* price subject to change

TO: THE SANDLAPPER STORE, INC.
P.O. Box 841
Lexington, South Carolina 29072

Please send me_____ copies of the **Southern Fish and Seafood Cookbook** at $4.95* per copy plus 75¢ per copy (for postage and handling). Orders for 5 or more books postpaid. S.C. residents add 4% sales tax to the cost of the books.

Name _____

Street _____

City _____

State & Zip_____

* price subject to change

TO: THE SANDLAPPER STORE, INC.
P.O. Box 841
Lexington, South Carolina 29072

Please send me _____ copies of the **Southern Fish and Seafood Cookbook** at $4.95* per copy plus 75¢ per copy (for postage and handling). Orders for 5 or more books postpaid. S.C. residents add 4% sales tax to the cost of the books.

Name _____

Street _____

City _____

State & Zip_____

* price subject to change